I have known Kam Wong and his wife, Gracia, for quite a number of years. He is a professionally qualified psychiatrist and a Christian with a deep and genuine personal faith. In this book, Dr. Kam skillfully explores the border where modern mental health therapy meets spirituality. He knows well the practice of modern psychiatry including the prescription of medications and counselling, but in treating patients suffering mental health problems due to stress and anxiety, Dr. Kam vividly describes cases where healing resulted because of trust in God and the invisible power of faith.

I was intrigued by how, in this book, Dr. Kam so clearly outlines the mental struggles many people face on a daily basis. As a pastor, I sometimes feel surrounded by people with psychological hurts. Our world is full of inner battles in which some people find victory, others are less successful, but everyone deals with at one time or another. In *Mental Health in Search of Spirituality*, Dr. Kam shows wisdom and insight into the Scriptures that give him, as a doctor, additional tools for healing the inner person of the mind. I recommend this book to everyone whose life work involves understanding and helping the people around them.

— **Peter Tsukahira**
Co-founding Pastor, Carmel Congregation, Israel

Mental Health in Search of Spirituality will be a welcomed addition for disciples of Jesus and church leaders alike who are seeking to grow in their understanding of the intersection between personal faith and the mental health issues that so many in our world face on a daily basis. Thought-provoking, insightful and thoroughly practical, this book combines profound Biblical truth with decades of clinical expertise in order to help believers experience the abundant life Jesus promised us. Those who read this will be greatly blessed!

— **James Wong**
Associate Pastor, Anchor Church, Sydney

Dr. Kam Wong has been a leading light as a psychiatrist and a Christian in helping children, adolescents, and their families find good mental health for over thirty years. We are fortunate that he has distilled his great expertise into his book, *Mental Health in Search of Spirituality*, which is filled with astute observations on not only why Christians are not immune to the challenges of living in this world, but also how both secular psychological/psychiatric treatment can partner with the Christian worldview to help us gain mental well-being. This is an important book for Christians, ministers and professionals alike and I am delighted to recommend this to all.

— **Dr. Terrance Lim**
Consultant Psychiatrist, Sydney

Mental Health in Search of Spirituality is a splendid contribution to one of today's most serious conversations concerning the connection between mental health and Christian spirituality. The excellent combination of Dr. Kam Wong's rich experience as a practicing psychiatrist and his faithful commitment to Christian faith and spirituality makes this book truly valuable for everyone—all psychiatrists who need to know what Christian spirituality has to offer, local pastors who accompany their church members struggling with their mental issues, and all Christians who tearfully walk in the darkness of the night. This book is scientifically based, theologically sound, and spiritually encouraging.

— **Joas Adiprasetya**
Jakarta Theological Seminary, Indonesia

Mental Health in Search of Spirituality is Dr. Wong's life's work. It's the culmination of years of clinical practice and authentically grappling with human suffering and a Christian response. This book masterfully synthesises complex topics and presents the reader with decades of wisdom in an easy-to-read format. As a friend and colleague, I can highly recommend this book.

— **Werner Teichert**
Clinical Psychologist, Sydney and South Africa

Dr. Kam Wong's *Mental Health in Search of Spirituality* is a transformative exploration of the vital connection between mental well-being and spiritual fulfillment. Drawing from his extensive background in child and adolescent psychiatry, Dr. Wong offers readers a profound understanding of mental health through cultural and spiritual lenses. This book not only enhances comprehension but also equips individuals with practical strategies to bolster their emotional and spiritual resilience. Filled with compassionate insights and actionable advice, it serves as an indispensable resource for anyone seeking to deepen their awareness of how spirituality can profoundly impact mental health and contribute to overall well-being. Discover a guide that empowers and enlightens, authored by a leading expert in the field.

— **Peter Tan**
Eaglesnest Kingdom Family, Malaysia

I have known Dr. Kam Wong for many years, and I highly esteem him for his spirit of excellence and deep commitment to the Word of God. In the past few decades, there has been a growing desire in the body of Christ for deeper understanding and a wholesome approach to the subject of inner healing. I believe Dr. Kam Wong makes a significant contribution in this book as a man proficient in medical practice with a solid grasp of biblical theology. I am excited to see this book published. It reminds me of the saying: "Nothing is more powerful than an idea whose time has come" (Victor Hugo).

— **Paul H.S. Kim**
Pastor of Glory International

In short, you hold in your hands a landmark book that presents a paradigm shift in how to approach mental illness. It provides a bridge integrating proven psychotherapy models with Christian spirituality. The integration of these two models I believe provides a more holistic path to healing for mental health sufferers than has ever been offered previously, and the excellent practical exercises alone make this book a 'must' purchase! Rest assured I will have a copy of this text on my bookshelf . . . the practical exercises alone are worth it—especially the steps in "Anchoring" oneself in the midst of acute anxiety, as well as learning the "Be still and know" steps which are absolute gold. But it's the exercises in the final chapter "Looking into the Father's Face" that are my favourite. They will now be included in my own regular spiritual disciplines (Thanks, Kam!). Anyone who suffers from fear or anxiety could safely apply these brilliant, yet simple exercises —and discover God's peace in the midst of them—possibly changing their life forever!

This book offers great hope for anyone who has mental health issues, because it prescribes a pathway showing how we can practically develop a deep and intimate relationship with Father God, who has always been the antidote to all our disorders.

— **Paul Ryan**
Centre Director for Ellel Sydney
Regional Director for Australia, Pacific and Indian Subcontinent

Mental Health
in Search of
Spirituality

TORN CURTAIN PUBLISHING
Auckland, New Zealand
www.torncurtainpublishing.com

ISBN Softcover 978-1-991299-27-7
ISBN EPub 978-1-991299-28-4

The content in this book is not intended as a substitute for professional psychological or psychiatric care, advice, diagnosis, or treatment of depression, anxiety, bipolar disorder, or any other mental health condition.

Some names and identifying details of people described in this book have been altered to protect their privacy.

Typeset in Yeseva One, Raleway, Minion Pro, Myriad Pro, Brittanic Bold

Cataloguing in Publishing Data
Title: Mental Health in Search of Spirituality: A Christian Psychiatrist's Understanding of Fear and Anxiety
Author: Dr Kam S Wong
Themes: Mental Health, Treatment of Psychaitric Disorders, Adjunct Psychiatric Treatments, Holistic Mental Health, Contemporary Societal Issues.
Subjects: Christian living, mental health, psychiatric disorders, anxiety disorders, Christian spirituality, counselling, depression, mental health and wellbeing, Obsessive Compulsive Disorder, Attention Deficit Hyperactivity Disorder, emotional wellbeing, biblical studies, faith-based psychotherapy, pastoral resources.

A copy of this title is held at the National Library of New Zealand.

Mental Health in Search of Spirituality

A CHRISTIAN PSYCHIATRIST'S UNDERSTANDING OF FEAR AND ANXIETY

DR. KAM S WONG

Contents

Kam Wong is a Malaysian-born Australian child, adolescent, and family psychiatrist in part-time private practice in Sydney. Being brought up partly in his formative years in Penang but having lived most of his life in Australia, Kam is a truly dual-cultural person. He speaks a number of languages besides English. Well-acquainted with the Confucian classics and the Judeo-Christian tradition, he is a fusion of the best of East and West.

Author's Note

Some years ago, I presented a series of talks on mental health to a Christian organisation. Realising the need for further discussion on the topic, I decided to follow up by writing a book, but due to the busyness of my practice, I had to put it aside after writing only two chapters. Had I continued at the time, that book would have been very different from the one you are reading today. Since then, I have journeyed further in my own understanding of Christian spirituality, gaining new insights and learnings which I have incorporated in my personal and professional life.

I was prompted to resume my unfinished task while teaching in the Far East and Southeast Asia. There, I noticed an increased prevalence of mental health problems like we have here in Australia. I also saw how mental health problems affect people irrespective of their religion. Christians are exposed to the same life stresses, uncertainties, troubled relationships, economic pressure, collateral damage from geopolitical conflicts, and trauma as those from any other faith. They suffer from the same degree of mental health problems as the rest of the population. But their Christian faith, which is foundational to their worldview, is barely addressed in the management and treatment of their mental health problems. This book seeks to address that deficiency.

I have written this book with the intention that it will be jargon- and psychobabble-free. It is not a psychiatric textbook. It is more a journey into my professional space as a psychiatrist and an invitation into my inner world of faith. Through this book, I hope you will gain a greater appreciation of how much Christian spirituality can offer the mental health sector, as well as a deeper understanding of mental health issues—regardless of whether or not you suffer with mental health challenges.

Be assured that I am not here as a disillusioned psychiatrist telling people that psychiatric treatment does not work, and psychological therapy is a waste of time. That is simply not true. But after thirty years of professional practice and being involved in the inner life and spirituality of my patients, I can say with confidence to both the medical profession and to Christian pastors that there is a more excellent way when it comes to the management of mental health.

I have been greatly blessed in writing this book. I hope you are greatly blessed reading it.

PART ONE

Mental Health and Spirituality

1

Mental Health in Our Society

We live in a world of increasing stress and anxiety, but thankfully there is also more awareness and openness regarding mental health problems—especially in the West—than ever before. Since the advent of the first antipsychotic medicine used to treat schizophrenia in the 1950s, neuroscientists and doctors have developed a vast range of medicines to use in mental health treatment. As a result, sufferers of mental health issues are less likely to experience discrimination than those who suffered in the previous century. Yet despite all these advancements and a greater awareness and care towards mental health, human beings are more stressed than ever.

THE PREVALENCE OF MENTAL HEALTH PROBLEMS

The term "stress" only started being applied in the context of mental health problems in the twentieth century. Hungarian medical doctor Hans Selye is often credited as a pioneer in the study of stress[1]. Prior to his observations in the 1930s, "stress" was a term more commonly used in the discipline of physical science. In studying the physical properties of various metals, scientists use pressures of varying severity to "stress" the metal in order to

---

1   Selye, H. (1936). *A syndrome produced by diverse nocuous agents.* Nature, 138 (3479), 32.

determine the exact point at which it will become distorted. In the same way that stress applied to metal causes drastic changes, stress applied to people causes a distortion of our humanity and our functioning. As a Christian psychiatrist, I believe that human beings are created in the image of God (Genesis 1:26, 2:7), and endowed by Him to be fully functional in our emotions, intellect, and will. Stress, however, causes a dysfunction in our abilities to lead an optimal life as intended by God. While stress is unavoidable in our modern world, we can begin to reclaim that optimal life by seeking to understand the nature and causes of human stress, how it affects us, and how we can best manage and even thrive despite it.

Standardisation of mental health classifications began in the Western world in the 1950s with the publication of the Diagnostic and Statistical Manual of Mental Disorders[2]. This has resulted in better recognition, diagnosis, and treatment of mental health problems. Even so, some mental health practitioners, including myself, believe that there has been an overall increase in the incidence of mental health problems over the last fifty years. Mental health experts are now identifying numerous mental health problems considered to be 'new kids on the block'. These include post-traumatic stress disorder (PTSD), complex post-traumatic stress disorder (C-PTSD), and autism spectrum disorder (ASD).

More recently, the World Health Organization recognised the impact of the Covid-19 pandemic on mental health, reporting a global increase in mental health problems as a result. The pandemic introduced various new stresses, including concerns about health, social isolation, economic hardships, and disruptions to daily life. These stresses have contributed to growing mental health struggles for many individuals and communities worldwide. In Sydney where I practise psychiatry, there is a mushrooming of mental health problems. Many mental health practitioners have a waiting list of twelve months or longer for new patient intake. Some have even closed

---

2   American Psychiatric Association, *Diagnostic and Statistical Manual of Mental Disorders (DSM-I)*. American Psychiatric Association, 1952

their books to all new referrals. It seems that, in Australia at least, mental health troubles are at an epidemic level.

In the two years prior to the Covid-19 pandemic, an estimated 14.3% of Australians aged eighteen to thirty-four reported high or very high levels of psychological distress—indicative of the level of anxiety and depression amongst that demographic[3]. In 2020-21, this figure rose to 20% (of Australians aged 16-34)[4]. Not surprisingly, suicide is an all-too-common cause of death within that age group. In fact, from 2019-2021, suicide was reported as the leading cause of death among Australians aged 15–24[5].

Self-harm, although it has a different root cause than suicide, seems to be also on the rise. While this is generally driven by a desire to release emotional pain and distress, rather than a wish to end one's life, self-harm is more common than we often perceive—particularly among young people. Many youths successfully conceal their struggle with self-harm by wearing clothes which hide evidence such as burns and laceration marks.

In my practice as a psychiatrist serving children, adolescents and families over the past thirty years, I have witnessed an increase not only in the prevalence but also in the complexity of mental health problems. When I first began training in psychiatry, clinicians were still using the previous generation's toolbox of antidepressant, antipsychotic, and mood-stabilising medicines. The arrival of the first "new generation antidepressant" (commonly known as *Prozac*) was greeted with much jubilation, and as young doctors in training, we hoped that prescribing the right medication would ultimately override the social and emotional factors that contributed to depression. However, this has not been the case. Despite the best diagnoses and treatment plans, stress, anxiety and depression have become more common than ever. It is now estimated that, at any point in time, 25% of the population in Australia has a diagnosable mental health problem. It is also true that up to

3 https://www.abs.gov.au/statistics/health/mental-health/national-study-mental-health-and-wellbeing/latest-release
4 https://www.abs.gov.au/articles/first-insights-national-study-mental-health-and-wellbeing-2020-21
5 https://www.aihw.gov.au/reports/life-expectancy-deaths/deaths-in-australia/contents/leading-causes-of-death

90% of the consultations conducted by primary family physicians are related directly or indirectly to some underlying mental health issue.

In other words, the majority of our physical diseases and problems are directly connected to mental health issues—whether the patient openly shares their mental state with their doctor or not. An astounding number of mental health problems masquerade as aches and pains of various kinds, the most notable of which is back pain. Additionally, people who suffer from ongoing health problems such as chronic pain are much more likely to suffer from anxiety and depression as well. It's a vicious cycle.

THE COMPLEXITY OF MENTAL HEALTH PROBLEMS

One of the greatest shifts I've noted throughout my career has been the increasing difficulty of treating mental health problems. When I first began working as a psychiatrist, it was rare to have patients taking more than one antidepressant or mood-stabilising medicine. These days, patients may take multiple medications for the same disorder. Practitioners who prescribe numerous medications for mental health problems are no longer frowned upon or considered incompetent. Instead, there is a recognition that more complex mental health issues call for a more complex approach to treatment.

This is particularly evident in the treatment of patients with attention deficit hyperactivity disorder (ADHD) and even high-functioning autism (ASD Level 1). In the past, I could submit a request for special educational support for my young patients, based on a singular diagnosis of the disorder. These days, I cannot guarantee that those same patients would qualify for help. This is not because the Department of Education has suddenly become more hard-hearted, but because those with more "complicated" mental health problems, such as anxiety and depression, far exceed those with a "simple" diagnosis such as ADHD or ASD Level 1. The reason is that today's children and adolescents with ADHD very often have associated mental health problems of anxiety and depression, and when there are only so many resources to go around, supporting those with more complex diagnoses becomes the priority.

During my psychiatric training, my professors taught that mental health problems such as anxiety and depression were time-limited disorders, whereas schizophrenia was a lifelong affliction. However, this view has also changed drastically. Talk to any mental health practitioner today, and they will tell you that there is an increase in both the complexity and severity of mental health problems. In fact, many of us have patients who seem to be resistant to treatment altogether, no matter what we try. Mental health problems are on the rise, and they are becoming more resistant too. Like many of my colleagues, I see a number of patients who struggle with chronic depression and anxiety. They take their medicine regularly, attend counselling and psychotherapy faithfully, and look after their health dutifully. Yet full remission of their depression and anxiety still eludes them. I have great respect for them and their courage to soldier on in life, despite their ongoing struggle and the seeming never-ending aspect of it.

While depression and anxiety are the two "mainstream" mental illnesses in our society, we will focus on anxiety rather than depression in this book. The complexity and methods of treatment for depression require a separate book. Instead, we will discuss the two-sided issue of *anxiety* and *fear*.

Now you may well ask, "Why another book on anxiety and fear? Aren't there too many of these in stores and libraries already?" Indeed, much has been written about fear and anxiety from a medical, clinical, psychological, and even lay perspective. But my hope is that I can bring a new perspective—the spiritual perspective. Many consider matters of the mind to be quite separate from matters of the spirit. My belief is that they are not so categorically separate. Whilst not synonymous, there is enough of an overlap that one clearly affects the other, and vice versa. In fact, recent studies have shown that one's spirituality does not only impact one's mental health problems but also one's *recovery* from these. Generally speaking, patients whose spirituality is acknowledged and accepted as part of their treatment, regain their health and functioning faster than those who don't.

MENTAL HEALTH PROBLEMS AND SPIRITUALITY

Outside my profession as a child, adolescent and family psychiatrist, I also offer Christian pastoral care. In praying for the sick and ministering to their concerns, I have come to further appreciate the importance of spirituality on our mental health. I have also observed that mental health problems are no respecter of persons. Christians and non-Christians alike suffer the same struggles with mental health. We all exist in the same world, and we are all impacted by changes in this world.

While changes help us learn to adapt and accommodate, they can also be stressful. Uncertainty during times of change often results in anxiety, and because anxiety negatively impacts our mental health, change is sometimes avoided or feared.

Interestingly, I have observed that it is my Christian patients, friends and acquaintances who struggle more with the concept of mental health. Many of my non-Christian patients are deeply religious and spiritually aware, but they do not feel the same tension between mental health and their personal beliefs. They seem better able to accommodate the idea of faith and mental health in the same room, they are more likely to seek help earlier, and they are more compliant in adhering to treatment. On the other hand, my Christian patients are more likely to have an antagonistic view of mental health, delaying seeking help and dropping out of treatment prematurely. But what causes this aversion to mental health care and all it entails?

Most of my Christian patients are referred to me by word of mouth. Others have heard me speak at mental health seminars or Christian conferences. I do not advertise myself solely as a Christian psychiatrist, but I am open about my faith and do not hide it. Consequently, I see many Christians in my practice.

I can therefore state with conviction and experience that having a Christian faith does not immunise us against stress and anxiety. It does not prevent us from suffering adverse childhood events, a poor upbringing, exposure to trauma, or making wrong choices in life. These life events can happen to anyone, making a person more vulnerable to developing mental health problems regardless of their faith.

Still, studies have shown that religious faith of any kind generally confers a better prognosis on those who suffer from mental health problems (though, as we have seen, it does not prevent mental health problems from arising in the first place). For Christians, this hope for recovery and ultimately overcoming the illness is founded in their relationship with Jesus, and consistent with what He said:

I have told you these things, so that in me you may have peace. In this world you will have trouble. But take heart! I have overcome the world.
— *JOHN 16:33*

Psychiatry is a very special profession. As a psychiatrist, I get to journey closely with my patients, often across an extended period in their lives. During this time, a therapeutic bond is formed, allowing me to offer hope in their battle to overcome mental health problems. It is my privilege to learn from my patients as much as they learn from me. I admire the courage of the many who persevere until they prevail, and I share in the joy of their victories just as much as I feel the agony of their distress. I have witnessed patients who have improved upon taking medication, others who have refused medication but gained victory through counselling and psychotherapy, and still others who have walked through a personal application of spirituality to mental health, to finally arrive at a place of healing.

Still, I believe there is a more excellent way to integrate Christian spirituality into mainstream practice. Medication and counselling or psychotherapy are beneficial, but when we integrate Christian spirituality, we bring a more holistic approach to mental health. It is from this perspective that I write this book, offering a fresh assessment that I hope will drive better outcomes for those we treat.

In John 10:10, Jesus announced:

The thief comes only to steal and kill and destroy; I have come that they may have life and have it to the full.

This book is about experiencing abundant life in the midst of our mental health problems. It is about the journey to get there despite those problems. It is also about exploring the concept, potential outcomes, and even case studies, of pairing traditional mental health treatments with the Christian faith.

But before we move on, let's revisit a question raised at the very beginning of this chapter: Why are mental health problems on the rise?

2

Why the Increase in Mental Health Problems?

Most mental health professionals would agree there has been a recent increase in mental health problems. However, it is difficult to exactly measure that increase. The main reason for this is that it is only in the last seventy years that psychiatrists and psychologists have had access to a more standardised "language" with which to describe mental health disorders. The advent of the first *Diagnostic and Statistical Manual of Mental Disorders* only came about in 1952. However, despite the lack of clear vocabulary around the subject at the time, the discipline of modern psychiatry can be traced back to the late 18th or early 19th centuries.

It was Sigmund Freud, the father of psychoanalysis, who began to turn the tide of understanding and interest around modern psychiatry, greatly influencing the study and treatment of mental disorders. Freud emphasised the existence of the unconscious mind and the role of early childhood experiences in shaping our adult behaviour. He believed that mental health problems were the result of conflicts within our psyche. He also developed the idea that neurosis is rooted in our unconscious conflicts and early childhood experiences. As a result, certain conditions that had traditionally been thought of as mental illnesses were no longer classified as mental health problems, while other conditions were more accurately named and identified. For example, by the mid-20th century, almost 100 years after Freud's work had begun the global conversation around psychoanalysis, the diagnosis of "anxiety" became more widespread, replacing the more generic term of "neurosis". World War II veterans who suffered from mental health problems had, at the time, been deemed to be suffering from "shell shock" or "war neurosis". These days, we agree that they probably suffered from post-traumatic stress disorder (PTSD).

Despite the difficulty in qualifying and quantifying mental health and wellbeing over an extended period, I, like many of my colleagues, believe that mental health problems have been on the increase since we first started our careers in this field.

There are many reasons that could account for this. Most, if not all, include the rapid environmental and societal changes that have taken place in our generation—changes that outpace our ability to adapt or cope. Changes in our environment as a society, whether positive or negative, normally result in a feeling of uncertainty. They require people to replace their old paradigm with a new one, in order to function well in their daily life. Too many of these changes—or changes occurring in swift succession—can quickly overwhelm our sense of stability and control.

Reflecting on my career over the last thirty years or so, I can offer several specific and plausible reasons as to why mental health problems are on the rise:

TECHNOLOGICAL ADVANCEMENT

It took me a long time to get used to this digital age we now live in. I belong to a generation brought up in a largely analogue world, and I was already in my late teens when I had to adjust to a digital environment. I remember the days of cassette tapes and recorders, VHS magnetic tapes, DVDs, and the subsequent shift to direct streaming. I have experienced the transition from Walkman to Discman to iPod to Spotify. I learned to adapt to the digital world, but it took some time before I felt comfortable with online banking. I preferred to receive a physical bill, write a paper cheque, or pay in cash and watch someone stamp my bill to say it had been "PAID". These are minor changes which we have accepted in our society and which are presumed to be positive because they increase efficiency and make life more streamlined. Even so, I still prefer to stroll into a shop where I can see, touch, feel and handle the merchandise rather than purchasing online. I have no way of telling if a restaurant serves good food, simply by looking at their Instagram page. For these sorts of decisions, I am totally dependent on my adult children who navigate this digital era with the ease of those born into it.

As advantageous as it may be, the advent of the digital age brought with it a mental health concern unique to the human civilisation of this present era. I have seen numerous patients whose lives have been negatively affected by inappropriate and excessive use of the internet. This problem is not confined to children and adolescents; it is also widespread among adults. Whilst internet addiction is yet to be listed in the *Diagnostic and Statistical Manual of Mental Disorders*—the accepted classification and diagnostic tool currently used by psychiatrists worldwide—these patients are clearly showing signs of obsession. People with social anxiety problems are particularly prone to this compulsion, as the internet provides an alternative "reality" for them. But in turn, this makes their social anxiety in the real world much worse. This struggle is particularly obvious with neurodiverse people, such as those with autism spectrum and attention deficit hyperactivity disorders. The social isolation and withdrawal that come as a result of immersion in the virtual world of technology, further exacerbate the social relationship problems of neurodiverse people.

Paradoxically, social media isolates rather than connects people. Meaningful relationships—which promote mental health and protect against mental issues—are rarely built in cyberspace but rather in the interpersonal space shared between individuals. Humans are relational beings, and life flourishes within collaborative experiences and mutual support. There is no greater joy than the sharing of laughter. Grief too is lessened when pain is shared. Even a smile from a stranger is enough to spark your own. Conversely, a text, an emoji, and even a GIF, give us little clarity as to the actual current experience and emotions of the sender. People frequently post glimpses of their lives on social media, waiting anxiously for a positive response—a thumbs-up, a hug icon, a smiley face, clapping hands—and reacting with genuine despondency when the response is not as anticipated. Without an invitation via social media, many young people spend their weekends in loneliness. Worse still, social media is an easy means for bullying, ostracism and ridicule to spread. I have treated too many young people who have such severe social anxiety and depression that they have resorted to self-harm to deal with the pain. Some of them have even overdosed in an attempt to block out the overwhelming fear and hurt. To my relief, none of those under my care have lost their lives in this way. But I see "cyberbullying" as a new and dangerous phenomenon; one which creates immense emotional distress and mental health concerns for this generation.

Thankfully, most of the teenagers I have treated do rediscover and begin to enjoy their life offline, after a period of counselling. My approach is not rocket science. Apart from offering counselling towards problem-solving their struggles and managing personal issues, I simply come alongside these teenagers; understanding the agony they feel over their isolation, affirming their need for acceptance, and introducing them to wholesome and pro-social group activities such as a local church youth group or a community scout program. Affiliation with a group like this is life-giving for humans, nourishing us on a spiritual, emotional and social level. Such benefits, like being included and accepted, cannot be overstated.

GLOBALISATION

Globalisation is another recent societal shift that has had a particular impact on many family units. My current practice is located in a relatively affluent part of Sydney, Australia. Many parents in this community have high-end jobs which require travelling to other countries throughout the year. The companies they work for are no longer confined to a single country; their executives and managers now service an entire region, for example, Asia Pacific. It is not uncommon for these executives to spend up to six months per year overseas, missing milestone events and formative years in the lives of their offspring. Consequently, their children struggle to form meaningful connections with their hard-pressed parents, and these young people often end up with significant mental health problems. Unfortunately, their easy access to a high disposable income further makes them vulnerable to the use of illicit substances. Being a therapist for these young people often involves adopting the role of a parent figure, offering sound and helpful advice and working with them through their developmental and interpersonal problems.

On a larger scale, globalisation has resulted in the creation of a "global village" but without the benefits of actual connections. Many people work across different time zones, and the trend towards working from home has led to a blurring of personal spaces and workspaces. One person might log off at the end of the working day, only to log back online after hours to connect with a customer in a different country halfway around the world. Another person could be part of a work team spread across states or even countries. Australia is part of the Asia Pacific Region, which means a person here could find themselves working alongside a team of colleagues who are based in China, Japan, Southeast Asia and India. This vast spread of a company's personnel can be quite detaching and demoralising for the individual, which in turn predisposes us to developing mental health problems. Even simple social opportunities such as catching up during morning tea or wishing one another a good weekend, help people to build positive relationships within the work environment, promoting good mental health.

I have personally treated patients who struggle with anxiety disorders as a direct result of being a solitary employee in a global team. One such case is a digital media architect who works locally in Sydney for a company based in London. Another also works locally but reports to their parent company in Europe. Both patients developed a propensity for panic attacks whilst working in isolation from the rest of the team, without any interpersonal connection. They also suffered constant doubts about their work performance.

Interestingly, not long after they quit their jobs, the panic attacks stopped. These two cases highlight the strong need for humans to be in meaningful, physical connection with others. Without that level of connection, we can end up losing a sense of our shared humanity.

In the movie "Cast Away", the main character, Chuck Noland, finds himself stranded on a deserted island following a plane crash. To survive his profound feelings of isolation and loneliness, Chuck paints a face on a volleyball and names it "Wilson". Over time, Chuck forms a deep emotional connection with "Wilson", desperately and futilely seeking companionship where there is none. Perhaps, this is why God created Eve for Adam and Adam for Eve (Genesis 2:18). Humans need proximity in their connection with other humans.

Globalisation has brought a level of awareness and interconnectedness that our world has never seen before. But ultimately, we are created to know one another on a personal, individual level. And this basic need for closeness and camaraderie is something globalisation can never satisfy.

CLIMATE CHANGE

We live in an age of unprecedented uncertainty, largely due to the dual explosions of information accessibility and global communication that arrived with the internet. One trending topic that causes much angst is the subject of climate change and the subsequent global warming that is impacting Earth. The debates rage back and forth as to whether there is such a phenomenon as climate change, and whether global warming is a result of the use of fossil fuel. Controversies abound as the debate for possible solutions continues. As a general population, we find it hard to cope with the prospects of a rising sea level, the destruction of marine life, unpredictable weather events, and the threat of our own survival on this planet.

Children and young people are even more affected by these global catastrophes, taking the very possible extinction of life as an imminent phenomenon. I have treated patients as young as seven years old, who have presented with anxiety and depression around this matter. One such patient was clearly unhappy, severely anxious, and socially withdrawn. In my first session with him, I asked him to tell me what his top three wishes would be—a gentle tactic that allows me to access the inner thoughts and unconscious mind of a child. The very first wish of this seven-year-old boy was for the world to end up with "no climate change so that my family will live". It turned out that the father of one of his friends is an environmental scientist who is working in conservation. Prior to this young child developing anxiety and depression, his friend had filled him in on the topic so many of us adults toss around and debate without a second thought—climate change.

In fact, I have many child and adolescent patients who are severely affected by "climate anxiety". Jessica (not her real name) is a neurodiverse patient of mine. I first saw Jessica when she was just six years old. At that time, I diagnosed her with autism spectrum disorder. She has been under my care since, and it has been my privilege to watch her grow up and to assist her in navigating a world which is often unsettling for those with this disorder. But during a recent review appointment, Jessica's mother reported that her twelve-year-old daughter had become more anxious in recent months. As well as heightened anxiety, Jessica had also developed the compulsive behaviour of checking house doors numerous times at night. Without these obsessive checks, she was unable to sleep peacefully. During our session, Jessica informed me that she would not live beyond the age of twenty-four years. She insisted that life on this planet would be extinct in twelve years' time. When I asked her for the reasoning behind her new belief, she explained that she had worked through some complicated mathematical calculations to arrive at her conclusion. Nothing could change Jessica's mind about the validity of her prediction, and it was only when I increased the dose of her medication that she became less anxious. Fortunately, this reduction of her anxiety has both lessened her mental agony over environmental issues and freed up her brain to learn new strategies with which to overcome her compulsive behaviours.

Climate change is a necessary conversation, and it is commendable that our generation is intent on doing our part to preserve the beauty of our planet and to ensure the sustainability of our environment for generations to come. Unfortunately, however, much of the activism and messaging around climate change is based on guilt and fear, both of which are detrimental to our mental health. Furthermore, the subject of climate change is often politicised. During election campaigns, politicians often hijack a debate with climate change proclamations and promises, to win votes. Too often this results in anger, fear and guilt spreading among the general population. Politicians who drive certain policies too harshly can often leave specific segments of the population feeling targeted and brutalised. Farmers for example are forced to bear the financial cost of net-zero emissions, resulting in great losses and the eventual shutting down of many farms. No wonder there is so much anger, stress, and anxiety in the community when it comes to climate change.

WARS AND RUMOURS OF WARS

Many people say human civilisation is built upon wars, and I think this statement is true. Here in Australia, a high school student who chooses the subjects of ancient history or modern history, invariably studies the history of wars. In the case of ancient history, this includes the Peloponnesian War; and in the case of modern history, this includes World War II, the Arab-Israeli Conflict, the Vietnam War, and the American Civil War. Even the Bible, which provides the foundation of the Judeo-Christian beliefs, contains many war narratives in both the Old and New Testaments. The people of God, as recorded in the Bible, lived through conflicts with great powers such as Egypt, Assyria, Babylon, Persia, Greece, and Rome. It seems that wherever there are humans, there are wars.

War and images of war are never pleasant, leaving an indelible mark on our psyche and our spirit. Eight years ago, my family and I visited Vietnam for a holiday. There, we visited the War Museum and the Chu Chi Tunnels in Ho Chi Minh City. Being confronted by visual images of the Vietnam War helped deepen my understanding of the atrocities inflicted upon the

Vietnamese people. My respect for the resilience of the Vietnamese people increased by a hundred-fold, and my new insight also helped me to better understand our own Australian Vietnam veterans. I had previously treated veterans hospitalised with post-traumatic stress disorder and had studied the Vietnam War and its destructive effects from a medical textbook. But the knowledge I gained did not really affect me in a tangible way until I visited Vietnam in person. Only then did the horrors of that war sink into my psyche, and I wondered how different my life would have been if I had lived in Vietnam at that time.

In the past, war was a distant event in a far-flung land, unless of course it occurred in our own country. But technology has brought the harsh reality of war into our personal spaces. In the 1960s and 1970s, television was available in most developed nations, creating a space where we could be exposed to war within our own homes. With the advent of the internet, that place of exposure can now be anywhere—even in the palm of our hands, as we hold an iPhone or a tablet. We now receive news at the speed of light. What happens in one small corner of the world can be known almost immediately, with stories and images instantly being uploaded online. War is now something that fills our workplaces, homes, public spaces and personal devices, as it plays out in front of us in real time.

Even slight exposure to war can lead to post-traumatic stress disorder. Repeated exposure through digital media can therefore inflict vicarious trauma, even upon those who are not directly experiencing war. One example of this is the Russian-Ukraine War which is ongoing at the time of writing. Whilst this war remains largely confined to Europe, it quickly became a world affair. Politicians around the globe weighed in with their opinions; nations were urged to take sides for or against Russia or Ukraine; geopolitical experts added their voices to the fray. And all of a sudden, YouTube and other social media platforms were overrun with alternative media channels attracting their own following. The looming spectre of World War III now lurks in our collective psyche, with talk of nuclear warfare becoming more prolific, and other situations around the world becoming more volatile.

As I write this book, talk of China imminently invading Taiwan has surfaced in the media. In Australia, some politicians are concerned about the ascendency of China. Some consider this to be part of an inevitable shift in the geopolitical balance of great powers. Many are anxious for their own and their children's futures. They feel that, by changing our foreign and defence policies, our politicians will make war with China even more inevitable. Talks and images of warships, submarines and naval exercises in the South China Sea only escalate and compound the anxiety and fear.

The reality of war often evokes fear and existential anxiety in people, and Christians are no exception. In fact, many Christians seem to be particularly affected by outbreaks of war and rumours of wars. Perhaps this is because of Jesus' words in Matthew 24:6, where He explains that His coming and "the end of the age" will be preceded by such events.

You will hear of wars and rumors of wars, but see to it that you are not alarmed. Such things must happen, but the end is still to come.

From this, we can conclude that Jesus never intended that war should strike fear and anxiety in people's minds. However, my perception is that Christians often lack the sense of security Jesus offers. Among Christians, we see varying emotional responses to the issue of wars and rumours of wars. Some have a passive resignation about the inevitability of such events and feel that they can do nothing about it. Others become quite anxious and fearful, preoccupied with whether they would survive an apocalyptic-style war. Yet others cope by reminding themselves that whenever the curtain finally falls, God has promised a better future.

Jesus, however, never intended that wars and rumours of wars should leave us feeling hopeless or afraid. In John 16:33, He acknowledges that "in this world we will have trouble." But when we read further, we find that His desire is that we should have peace—and hope.

*I have told you these things, so that **in me you may have peace**. In this world you will have trouble. **But take heart! I have overcome the world.***

Hope helps us to transcend earthly circumstances and see our distress and suffering as a temporary experience. This is why Christian spirituality is so important. It allows us to view war and rumours of war from another perspective. The ability to endure even the most traumatic events increases when we find our hope and security in Christ.

THE COVID-19 PANDEMIC

Another factor affecting the mental health of people worldwide in our generation has been the Covid-19 pandemic. In recent years, there has been a significant exacerbation of mental health problems in those with preexisting diagnoses, and new mental health problems in those without a prior diagnosis. Ever since the global virus hit, we have seen an increase in the incidence of anxiety, depression, substance abuse, self-harm, suicide, and truancy among students. Younger children are also exhibiting delays in their developmental process. Though the world has learnt to live with the virus, the consequent mental health problems and effects are still ongoing.

People who were infected, or were suspected of being infected, with the Covid-19 virus, suffered intense emotional distress including high anxiety and fear. Images of sick patients in intensive care units being intubated and connected to the ventilators sparked a visceral fear of death. Those who were hospitalised suffered a profound sense of isolation and the fear of dying alone. Loved ones who were unable to visit patients in hospital were also distressed and often overcome with fear, guilt, and anger. Extreme social isolation, which was adopted to prevent the spread of the virus, resulted in mental health problems—such as anxiety and depression—skyrocketing. Many people resorted to excessive use of alcohol and other substances to quell their emotional distress. Loss of employment, perception of governmental overreach in enforcing quarantine measures, controversies over the vaccines, and the loss of autonomy over one's health decisions, resulted in intense anxiety, anger, and fear. Enduring lockdown measures and social restrictions led to increased stress and depression, particularly in the more vulnerable age groups such as young people and the elderly.

Many of my elderly patients are still recovering from the pressure and anxiety they encountered because of the Covid-19 lockdown. One woman, whom I will call "Mary", was functioning well before the pandemic. A single lady who lived alone, her daily schedule was rigidly mapped out to include healthy routines, fun outings, and social gatherings. She began each day with a morning walk, followed by a light breakfast and a cup of coffee at the local café. Her afternoons were taken up with helping to run an English class in a local church for speakers of other languages, meeting up with her friends, or doing shopping and running errands. In the evenings, she would spend time reading and enjoying phone calls with her nephews and nieces. But as a direct result of the Covid-19 lockdown, Mary suffered from severe anxiety and depression. The isolation, fear, and uncertainty proved too much, and she did not recover from these mental health struggles, despite vigorous treatment. She became so stressed that, after a while, she was no longer able to look after herself, let alone teach English or check in on friends. Mary has since been admitted to an aged care facility, no longer enjoying an active life as her bubbly, confident self.

A significant number of my younger patients had been diagnosed with neurodiversity such as autism and attention deficit hyperactivity disorder. Others had not yet received a professional mental health diagnosis, but post-pandemic, they had one thing in common: they struggled to attend school full-time and were eventually diagnosed with social anxiety disorder. These students were not slack. They were not lazy. They were literally too anxious to go to school. Most had a deep fear of "catching Covid", and as none of them coped well with online schooling and being isolated from instructors and peers, they began lagging behind in their learning, and many felt ashamed of being "dumb".

The true extent of the long-term mental health effects of the Covid-19 pandemic has yet to be determined. It is estimated that there has been a staggering 25% increase in stress, anxiety, depression and substance abuse since the pandemic. But we also know that mental health problems are notoriously difficult to detect, meaning the numbers could in fact be much higher. Many suffer silently due to shame and despair. Often those with mental health problems that are masked by other conditions such as substance abuse—a self-medicating attempt to alleviate their underlying emotional distress—do not seek help for fear of being labelled an addict. Meanwhile, they often have undiagnosed mental health issues such as anxiety and depression. While the pandemic arguably brought out the best in humanity, it also uncovered our deepest vulnerabilities. The psychological impact of the Covid-19 pandemic has been felt by nearly every person in this era, and the effects and subsequent fallout are likely to be felt for generations to come.

DECONSTRUCTION

Finally, anxiety as an outcome of environmental change is occurring because we are living in an age of deconstruction. This philosophy emerged in the 20th century through the work of the French philosopher Jacques Derrida. Deconstruction is a big topic, beyond the scope and purpose of this book. As far as I know, the main tenet of deconstruction is the emphasis on subjectivity and the challenge of fixed meaning around language and concepts. Deconstruction asserts that language and concepts are ambiguous, subject to interpretation and context. It challenges binary opposites such as good and evil, black and white. It challenges the idea of the absolute. Deconstruction has a far-reaching influence in various areas of our lives, including education, societal structure, interpretation of history, religions, arts, literature and mental health.

In a nutshell, deconstruction is a method of analysis and interpretation in the quest for meaning. The importance of meaning cannot be overstated for human beings. Each one of us faces a time in our lives, especially during our teenage years when we ask ourselves two questions: "How did I come to be?" and "Why am I here?" Pondering these questions leads us to examine our upbringing, culture, traditions, religious beliefs, values, and family practices. As we grow in understanding, we keep that which we deem relevant and meaningful to us, leaving behind anything we feel no longer fits our narrative, and incorporating new perspectives into our personal belief system.

Within that system are many ideas we might consider absolute, enduring and unchanging, such as our belief in God, certain moral codes, and how we treat one another in our relationships. Our life is guided, consciously or unconsciously, by our personal belief system. It is the compass which influences our behaviours and direction throughout life's journey. Having a strong belief system helps to provide a sense of certainty about life and ourselves, which reduces anxiety and fear.

Some of us, however, don't cope well with deconstruction. When a new layer of understanding is exposed, we feel as though the rug has been pulled out from under our feet. We can feel afraid to enter this new and unchartered territory, as all that used to be familiar suddenly seems strange and uncertain. Some even feel that deconstructing a previous idea means they never truly grasped the entity in the first place. Whatever they thought they were dealing with must not have been true after all. The resultant feelings of uncertainty and loss of control can culminate in further anxiety problems.

As human beings, we crave a sense of continuity. We need a connection to our past—in fact, we can only know where we are today by anchoring ourselves in the events of yesterday and the day before. Our past locates us and provides a reference to our ongoing lives. Without it, we land in a state of existential crisis. Transient global amnesia (TGA) is a medical condition in which the individual suffers memory loss for a few hours, with no ability to recall recent events. During an episode of transient global amnesia, a person becomes disoriented, confused and fearful because of the loss of continuity in their personal history and meaning. A society finds itself in crisis—and therefore more at risk of mental health issues—when there is a collective loss of memory or continuity because of intentional deconstruction.

When we begin to think that everything is relative, we are left without absolutes and therefore in a state of constant uncertainty. If we applied deconstruction to any other science, the laws of the universe would break down. For example, in the realm of physical science, we accept that the speed of light is absolute and unchanging. With that as a reference point, the universe makes sense to us. If we deconstructed Newton's Laws, our understanding of the universe would break down. But when it comes to human science, we are less inclined to accept absolutes. We prefer to believe that everything about the human experience is relative. Deconstruction in human science creates even more instability, leaving us without absolutes to anchor ourselves to, and therefore in a state of constant anxiety and uncertainty.

~

All these phenomena—*technological advancement, globalisation, climate change, wars and rumours of wars, the Covid-19 pandemic, deconstruction*—impact us collectively and as individuals, either directly or indirectly. They challenge our sense of security, both intellectually and—worse—existentially. As a species, we feel less empowered, less certain about life, and less in control. No wonder we have become more stressed, more anxious, and more depressed.

3

The Multi-Dimensional Aspect of Mental Health

The World Health Organization defines mental health as "a state of well-being in which every individual realizes his or her own potential, can cope with normal stresses of life, can work productively and fruitfully, and is able to make a contribution to his or her own community"[6]. In other words, mental health is a state of emotional, psychological, and social well-being. It determines how we feel, think, and behave. It affects how we handle stress, how we achieve our potential in life, and how we approach our relationships with others. It also impacts our productivity and our ability to contribute to the community in which we live.

But what happens when our mental health is compromised? We all face problems such as stress, fear, injury and trauma, so what constitutes a mental health problem or disorder?

---

6 World Health Organization. *Promoting mental health: concepts, emerging evidence, practice* (Summary Report) Geneva: World Health Organization; 2004.

A PSYCHIATRIC DISORDER IS A
BIOPSYCHOSOCIAL DISORDER

To understand mental health disorders, we first need to shift our paradigm away from how we view physical illness. There are vast differences between physical and mental problems. While physical illness is measured with scans, blood tests, spirometry etc., mental illness is measured primarily in terms of a person's ability to function optimally. For example, if a professor can no longer fulfil his academic role due to depression or anxiety, instead becoming a part-time tutor, he is no longer operating at his optimal capacity—despite still working in his field. Or consider the mother who manages to get her children ready for school and drops them off at the school gate on time, but then goes home to lie down for most of the day before rising later that afternoon to pick them up again. Clearly, this mother is not functioning optimally, despite her ability—and the hard work she puts in—to keep caring for her children.

Now let's presume this mother has been to her doctor for a health check, undergoing blood tests, scans, and other investigations. Her iron levels are normal, her thyroid is healthy, and there are no obvious diseases at play. In this case, there is a good chance this mother is struggling with a mental health issue. In the case of a physical illness, the disease process that occurs in the person's body can very often be shown through scans, blood tests or other physical investigations. But in order to understand mental health problems we need a different framework. Most mental health problems are recognised by a decrease in the daily functioning of the sufferers rather than a distinct disease process. While a scan or blood test may indicate association, we cannot establish causality at this stage. That is why the medical profession uses the term "disorder" to describe mental health problems rather than "illness" or "disease".

While some physical illnesses usually originate from a simple root cause, mental health problems are nearly always the final convergent point of many different factors. "But—" you may ask "—isn't depression caused by a lack of serotonin in the brain?" Well, to be strictly scientific, that is not quite true—even though most doctors would explain depression in this simplistic way when prescribing an antidepressant to a patient. We know that antidepressants increase the net amount of serotonin in the nerve cells, and therefore, by retrograde reasoning, we hypothesise that depression is due to a lack of serotonin in the brain cells. This is called the amine hypothesis of depression. But the relationship between depression and serotonin is more complex than a straightforward model of deficiency. In other words, mental health problems do not have a simple cause and effect. They are not caused by a single pathogen such as a virus, bacterium or fungus, or a single disease process such as blockage of arteries or atherosclerosis. Rather, mental health problems are a cumulation of biological, psychological, and social factors.

Biological Factors

In mental health, the genetic history of a patient's family plays a part in the development and diagnosis of mental health problems, as well as the choice of treatment. A family history of anxiety and depressive disorders makes it more likely—though not inevitable—that an individual will suffer from the same disorder. Psychiatrists call this increased propensity *genetic loading*. For example, the general population has a 1% risk of developing schizophrenia. But if a person has a parent who is affected by schizophrenia, that person's risk is increased to 10%. In addition, physical health problems such as thyroid or autoimmune diseases make an individual more susceptible to mental health problems.

Psychological Factors

Psychological factors such as our early upbringing, the parenting style we received, and our relationships with significant others (such as parents and other parental figures), can affect our mental health later in life. Children who do not feel secure in relationships with their significant carers are more prone to mental health problems—such as anxiety and depression—in their adulthood. Likewise, traumatic experiences such as abuse, neglect, abandonment, violence, and exploitation, leave an indelible mark on a child's psyche and make the victim more susceptible to mental health problems as they mature. Research also shows that early trauma affects the development of a child's brain, switching on responses such as hyper-alertness that often carry on or are triggered long after the cessation of the trauma.

One example of the longevity of trauma is illustrated in people of any age who find themselves in a tense situation and default to a fight-flight response. A person can experience trauma directly (as a victim) or vicariously (being an eyewitness). Sometimes trauma comes even when one is distanced from the traumatic event. Take for example the "9/11" tragedy, when terrorists hijacked and crashed two aeroplanes into the Twin Towers of the World Trade Centre in New York City on 11 September 2001. As a result of watching the video clip of the crash and its endless re-runs on television, many viewers suffered from vicarious post-traumatic stress disorder. I have even treated children and adults who have developed a fear of flying due to the vicarious trauma of "9/11".

Psychological factors affect all of us. Some of us are allowed the opportunity to process these in a healthy way, but others may not have access to the safe environment or stable situation needed to undergo such processing. The latter will therefore suffer the ongoing psychological effects of a negative experience long after it has taken place, and many will need professional help to process the trauma and strengthen their psychological resilience.

Social Factors

Humans are social beings. We do not and cannot exist by ourselves. We need others to express our true selves and to help us derive meaning in life, and we need healthy relationships with significant others in order to achieve and maintain good mental health. Research shows that babies nurtured by mothers with depression (who exhibit reduced facial expressions, a lack of spontaneity, and some level of withdrawal from their babies) are more likely to develop depression themselves. In fact, the babies may begin to mirror their mothers while still in infancy. In these situations, babies often grow up to become individuals with less robust mental health and more susceptibility to anxiety and depression. Our early life experience, particularly in regard to our carers, is a microcosm of our social life later on. Meaningful social connections give us a sense of belonging, support and significance, and increase our emotional resilience, even in times of struggle. On the other hand, a lack of social connection makes us more vulnerable to developing mental health problems, as we find ourselves cut off from the safety, support and meaning that community brings. It is little wonder that people who suffer from anxiety disorders often have an anxious attachment with their significant carers.

Given the above, a psychiatric diagnosis is only the first step in understanding our patients. We still need to go one step further to discover the biological, psychological, and social factors that are acting together to result in a mental health problem. Such a holistic understanding also helps us to customise a management plan for each individual patient. This is important, as no two individuals have the same biological, psychological, and social factors—even if the psychiatric label applied to both is the same. To illustrate, let me share some of my own cases with you.

CASE STUDIES

Robert Smith[7]

Robert is a fifty-five-year-old Christian who was referred to me by his general practitioner. He struggled with a considerable level of mental distress—in particular, the experience of intrusive thoughts and images, both of a sexual kind. He had never been a perpetrator, but these thoughts had impacted Robert to the point where, despite having been an honest and successful high school teacher for thirty years, he had now lost interest in his profession. Instead, he decided to open a printing business in his local suburb. Feeling that he was suffering burnout from his teaching profession, Robert had always wanted to be his own boss and to run a business. While

---

7   Not his real name

he felt he would have no problem running a simple printing business, he did not have enough money to start. So Robert borrowed capital from his brother, promising to repay him with interest and a share of the business once it became successful.

Unfortunately, Robert did not do well in his business. In an attempt to turn things around, he borrowed more money from his brother. However, the extra injection of funds did not help, and the business continued to deteriorate. The main reason for this downhill battle was Robert's lack of concentration due to his mental distress. He had continued to experience intrusive sexual thoughts, despite hoping these would cease once he resigned from his teaching profession. In addition, he was now feeling the pressure of not making a profit from his business, and guilty that he could not make a positive return on his brother's investment.

Prior to this mental health problem, Robert had never seen a psychiatrist or a counsellor. His physical health was good, and he was happily married. No one in his family had suffered from any mental health problems, and Robert himself was not on any long-term medication for physical illness or injury.

I diagnosed Robert with an anxiety disorder called obsessive compulsive disorder. I was confident that biological factors did not contribute to his disorder due to his clean bill of health and his family having no history of such struggles. He had a good relationship with his wife and had a large circle of friends, so the social factor did not play a role in his disorder. But Robert had entered a profession he didn't really enjoy. Simply going to work felt tedious for him, and this contributed to his subsequent burnout and anxiety.

I initially treated Robert with medication combined with psychological therapy. I prescribed a high-dose antidepressant medication which is normally used for obsessive compulsive disorder. Due to the severity of his anxiety disorder, I also added an antipsychotic medication.

I soon found out that Robert had a tremendous fear that he would act out the intrusive thoughts and images occurring in his head, in real life. This was most repugnant and shameful to him. I therefore provided further psychological therapy called cognitive behaviour therapy (CBT)—a well-known and effective treatment for anxiety and depressive disorders. The basis of CBT is the understanding that negative or irrational thought patterns give rise to negative or irrational emotions and behaviour. Accordingly, to change one's negative emotions and behaviour, one must first change the negative or irrational thought patterns. In Robert's case, my aim was to lead him to understand that thoughts are not reality and that he had full control over his own behaviour. I conducted a number of counselling sessions with Robert, helping him to identify negative or irrational thought patterns, challenge them, and finally replace them with more constructive thoughts.

As Robert is a Christian, I also encouraged him to be more involved in his church's activities, such as spending more time with men in whom he found a deep kindred spirit and by whom he felt emotionally supported. By so doing, I managed to use biological (medicine), psychological (psychotherapy), and social (church community) means to help Robert.

After six months, Robert had made good improvements, but his struggles were not yet fully managed. We had hit a glass ceiling, and I sensed there was more to his struggle with mental health. I decided to take a deeper look into his problems, and I will share more on this in chapter five.

Teresa Khoo[8]

Teresa was a 36-year-old teacher who had a known history of generalised anxiety disorder. She was a keen Christian who attended church regularly and ran a small weekly group with her husband. They now have an eight-year-old daughter. But soon after their daughter had turned seven, Teresa developed an obsessive fear of knives. Whenever she saw a knife, she was hit with a compulsive desire to stab someone. This compulsive desire was accompanied by intrusive images of how the stabbing would be carried out. To protect herself from her fear of knives and the associated impulse to stab someone, Teresa decided to lock away all the knives in their house. She also delegated the cooking to her husband. Whenever she did need to

---

8   Not her real name

cook, she would only use precut meat, for example minced or diced, so that she did not need to use a knife.

Teresa was referred to me because she felt more comfortable seeing a Christian psychiatrist. She was also concerned that a non-Christian doctor would simply think that she was mad. I diagnosed obsessive compulsive disorder and began treatment with an antidepressant medication which also has an anti-obsessive and anti-compulsive property. I also began cognitive behaviour therapy with Teresa, as it is the gold standard treatment of choice for OCD.

Teresa responded well to the combined modalities of medication and cognitive behavioural therapy. Soon, she was able to tolerate the sight of knives and to challenge her intrusive images of stabbing with greatly reduced anxiety. She was able to tolerate her fear and label it as irrational, without succumbing to her desire to lock the knives away. She was also able to use knives in her food preparation and cooking. However, after a while her improvement plateaued. Over time, her anxiety over knives would resurface, and her obsessive compulsive disorder relapsed whenever I attempted to reduce her medication beyond a certain level.

I decided to return to first base, to understand more of Teresa's history—especially her early childhood—and to look for potential root causes of her obsessive compulsive disorder. I learnt that she had been raised in an emotionally charged family due to her parents' tumultuous marital relationship which sowed chronic discord. Domestic violence abounded. Her father had an alcohol problem, and he would often come home drunk and behave aggressively towards Teresa's mother. But Teresa and her sister, who is two years her junior, were not spared either. From a young age, Teresa had learnt to stay out of her father's way by hiding in her room. She would make sure to keep her younger sister away from their father as well.

Teresa remembered wishing her father dead on many occasions. She even wished that she had a different father. One evening her father returned home very drunk. A fight ensued between her parents, and Teresa retreated to her bedroom as usual with her sister in tow. From behind their closed door, the two little girls heard shouting, screaming, and banging. They heard the familiar crashing of objects being thrown, and then there was a sudden gap of silence. Suddenly Teresa heard her mother shouting, "Don't you dare! Don't you dare!" Teresa opened her bedroom door and peered through the crack. She saw her father standing close to her mother with a kitchen knife in his hand. He was breathing heavily.

Teresa rushed out of the bedroom with her little sister. Their mother turned around and grabbed the children as their father spilled out threatening words. Everything happened so quickly that Teresa has no recall of the exact content of his threats. But she remembered her mother grabbing both children and running out of the house. Behind them, Teresa's father continued to shout threats. Teresa and her sister and mother ended up in her maternal grandparents' home that night. They stayed for some months, and Teresa remembered that it was there in her grandparents' home that she celebrated her eighth birthday. They never returned to their own home.

Teresa remembers not missing her own home, but instead appreciating the peace and quiet at her grandparents' home. She does not remember how old she was when her mother informed her that her father had passed away, but she did not attend the funeral. It was not until she turned eighteen that her mother shared the truth—her father had killed himself when Teresa was still only eight years old.

Knowing more of her childhood history, the dynamics of her family of origin, her difficult relationship with her father, and the circumstances around his death, I came to a different formulation of Teresa's obsessive compulsive disorder—namely her fear of using a knife to stab someone. I opined that she had internalised and repressed her anger and her death wish for her father. Her last memory of her father brandishing a kitchen knife at her mother had greatly traumatised her and was etched into her unconscious mind. His subsequent suicide fulfilled her death wish about her father. A knife had therefore become the link between her repressed distress and his death. Teresa's trauma and the associated emotions were largely buried in the deep recess of her unconscious mind until her own daughter turned eight—the same age Teresa had been when the finale of her childhood trauma occurred. I knew now that her obsessive compulsive disorder around knives, and her fear of stabbing people, were symbolic of her unresolved inner conflicts.

I guided Teresa through psychotherapy to explore her relationship with her father in a safe setting. I also offered her the space to confront her inner pain, anger, disappointment, and even her guilt that her death wish towards her father had somehow caused his demise. We processed forgiveness around her father, and Teresa forgave him for the domestic violence he brought into their home and for robbing her of a safe and happy childhood. Finally, she was also able to forgive herself for harbouring hatred towards him.

After resolving her negative emotions towards her late father, Teresa made greater improvements regarding her obsessive compulsive disorder. Unresolved feelings towards a person can surpass their lifetime, and this was the case with Teresa. Interestingly, despite these huge revelations and the subsequent improvements, Teresa still did not make a full recovery from her obsessive compulsive disorder. I felt there was still more to her trauma that we had not explored, and with her permission, Teresa and I took yet another journey into her innermost self, which I will share in chapter five.

THE LIMITATIONS OF A BIOPSYCHOSOCIAL APPROACH

Robert's and Teresa's stories clearly illustrate how a biopsychosocial approach works in psychiatry. Both patients had the same diagnosis: an anxiety disorder called obsessive compulsive disorder. Both were treated biologically with medication and psychologically with cognitive behavioural therapy. They each had a different psychological reason for their disorders, but the approach towards healing was the same and proved equally successful—at least to a certain point.

Understanding the psychological reasons for this disorder is one thing. Helping a patient to fully resolve the consequential psychological conflicts is another matter. I had brought in the biological, psychological, and social approaches for both Robert and Teresa, as is standard (and successful) as a practice. But there is another dimension which is just as real in a patient's life—the spiritual. This extra element is often neglected in the biopsychosocial approach, but it is a crucial intersection between mental health and spirituality. This is where the mind and the spirit intersect. It means acknowledging all the individual aspects that make a person whole. It means inviting the spiritual into the story of trauma and healing. Perhaps it also means a new, creative, more inclusive approach to psychiatry.

4

Psychiatry and Christian Spirituality

Human beings are infinitely complex. The difficulty in understanding our species is best conveyed in the story of *The Blind Men and The Elephant* by John Godfrey Saxe[9]. Six blind men, who have no prior knowledge of an elephant, attempt to identify it by feel alone. One touches the trunk and says an elephant is a thick snake. Another touches the body and declares it a wall, while the third touches the tail and says it is a rope. The fourth feels the ear and says an elephant must be a fan, while the fifth and sixth men decide it is a spear and a tree trunk respectively, after touching the tusk and legs. Each man has a partial and incomplete understanding of what an elephant is as a whole.

Like *The Blind Men and The Elephant*, psychology and psychiatry—the disciplines that study abnormalities of the mind—are limited in understanding the human mind and human behaviour. Fortunately, we are not totally blind and groping in the dark like the six blind men! Though our practice is based on an incomplete system of knowledge, there is still ongoing and ever-improving research into neuroscience and human behaviour. Understandably, there

---

9 Saxe, John Godfrey. "The Blind Men and the Elephant." *Poems of John Godfrey Saxe*, 1873.

is some confusion between psychology and psychiatry. Lay people tend to think that if you want counselling then you consult a psychologist, and if you want medicine then you see a psychiatrist. Some also assume that seeing a psychologist means the problem must not be too serious, but seeing a psychiatrist means "I must be losing my mind". This cannot be further from the truth, and there is a tangible distinction between the two disciplines.

Psychology is best understood as a discipline that belongs to the social sciences. It is the scientific study of behaviour and mental processes, seeking to understand how and why individuals think, feel, and behave in various situations. Psychiatry, however, is a medical specialty that deals with the diagnosis, treatment, and prevention of mental illnesses and disorders. As medical specialists, psychiatrists offer a biopsychosocial approach to the management of mental health problems, including medications when necessary, a range of psychological treatments or psychotherapy, and social intervention.

UNDERSTANDING THE MIND

It is estimated that, globally, there are over 400 types of psychological treatments and psychotherapies. Each school of psychotherapy offers its theory of the mind, proposing to gain insight into the person's thinking and behaviour. Each also makes certain explanations as to how psychological problems arise in a person's life. Accordingly, therapists trained through these schools will offer treatments to rid a sufferer of the root causes they have learned to identify, so that the person may gain freedom from their problems. For example, behaviour therapy posits that psychological problems arise as a result of negative behaviour. By challenging and correcting those negative behaviours, the problems can be overcome. However, pure behavioural therapy is often criticised for its "black box" approach; it sees human beings as the sum of behaviours and ignores or denies the existence of the unconscious mind.

When a person seeks counselling and psychotherapy, the therapist will seek to understand the nature of problems within the framework of their own theory of the mind. The therapist will formulate the reason why the problem has arisen in the person's life and offer a solution within the same framework of the therapist's understanding. For example, a behavioural therapist understands that a person's problem is largely due to unhelpful behaviour in the person's own life. They will therefore offer help in aiding the person to cultivate more positive behaviour. On the other hand, a cognitive behavioural therapist is more likely to formulate that unhelpful thinking styles are the root cause of a person's problems. This therapist will help their patient to identify unhelpful thinking styles, challenge them, and then replace them with more helpful thinking styles.

Some of the common psychotherapies include:

Psychodynamic psychotherapy which posits that anxiety is a result of unresolved inner conflicts within the patient. The root of such conflicts is usually located in the person's past experiences such as a formative period of one's development, e.g. early childhood. Successful resolution of these inner conflicts will result in the cessation of anxiety.

Cognitive behavioural therapy (CBT) which posits that our thoughts precede and drive our feelings. A person feels anxious because of anxious thoughts. By discovering the anxious thoughts, challenging them, and replacing them with non-anxious thoughts, a person is freed from the anxiety. The psychotherapist helps the person to detect, challenge and replace irrational thoughts with more rational thoughts by doing specific "homework" such as having a thought journal.

Dialectical behavioural therapy (DBT) which teaches the person skills on how to deal with intense emotions such as fear and anxious feelings by accepting and tolerating them. However, the patient is also taught skills to better regulate their emotions and improve their interpersonal communication, self-assertiveness, and self-worth. Dialectical behavioural therapy is commonly used for various mental health problems.

Acceptance and commitment therapy (ACT) encourages the person to embrace the anxious feelings and thoughts, rather than seeing them as noxious, terrible, and threatening. The person is also taught to make value-based decisions about their life and to commit to making changes so that they can be free of their mental health struggles.

~

Whenever you seek help from a therapist, it is important to check the background and training of that therapist so that you have a fair idea of how they will manage your problems. It is also helpful to make an initial appointment with the therapist to be sure you are confident to entrust that person with your mental health. It is important to take ownership of your own mental health. The reality is that while therapists are not supposed to impose their values on their patients, it is inevitable that their worldview will have some impact on those they treat. Asking questions such as *What do you think is wrong with me? What is the treatment plan for me?* will help you decide if the therapist is right for you.

I consider myself an eclectic psychotherapist. Psychodynamic theory, with its emphasis on early life and childhood experiences, helps me to understand how my patient has ended up with the type of problems they are facing. It also highlights my patient's unresolved and unconscious conflicts. However, I also draw from my training in cognitive behavioural therapy, dialectical behavioural therapy, and acceptance commitment therapy to help my patients.

In my practice, it is only after getting to know and understand a patient's problems that I will give them feedback and explain the management plan I think is useful. If I believe that psychological treatment or psychotherapy is warranted, I normally give the patient a trial of between three to five therapy sessions. During this time, there is an opportunity for an increase in mutual understanding of each other. The patient can decide if my level of expertise, my personality style and my approach to their struggles, are positive and helpful towards healing. Chemistry is as important as competence. At the end of the trial period, the patient is free to quit if they prefer, with no effort on my part to convince them otherwise.

WHY CHRISTIANS FIND IT HARD TO SEEK PSYCHOLOGICAL HELP

Over the years working as a clinician, I have observed that it is Christians more than non-Christians who have difficulty seeking psychological help. Christians are also more likely to feel stigmatised by having mental health problems. We believe that Jesus has come to offer abundant life (John 10:10), but living with mental health problems bears no semblance to the abundant life described in the Bible. So when a Christian suffers from a mental health issue, it is natural to land in a state of self-condemnation, berating themselves for things such as not being spiritual enough, not praying enough, or not spending enough time reading the Word of God. However, some Christians see mental health problems as "the thief that comes to steal, kill and destroy" (John 10:10). They become motivated to overcome the problem with a positive attitude and mindset.

Still, many Christians are reluctant to seek help for fear of being misunderstood by their therapist. They fear a therapist will not be sympathetic towards their Christian faith, and they are concerned that they will be actively challenged to give up their Christian faith. I am sympathetic towards this fear. The great majority, if not all schools of psychotherapies, do not accommodate the matter of God. In fact, the belief in God seems anathema to much of psychological thinking. Some therapists may tolerate it. Others consider it a dependency issue which hinders a person from achieving full autonomy and self-fulfilment. For many Christians who consider their Christian faith central to their life, this approach can lead to an existential crisis.

Some Christians consider mental health problems to be a manifestation of spiritual problems. Over the last twenty years or so, the concept of inner healing has become prevalent among Christians. Praying for the sick is a common Christian practice (James 5:14-15), and believers who are sick often seek out their pastors and lay leaders to minister to them through prayer. Some churches and Christian organisations set aside specific meetings for prayer ministry over the sick. To me, inner healing through prayer ministry is a type of therapy.

Therapy is the active healing of the inner person, the spirit and the psyche, as well as the processing and eventual laying down of associated negative thoughts, emotions, and painful and traumatic memories. The purpose of inner healing prayer is to set a person free from the burden of negative emotions such as resentment, guilt, depression, insecurity and feelings of worthlessness. This is often accomplished through forgiveness of oneself and others, correction of false beliefs, and sometimes deliverance from evil spirits.

Practitioners of inner healing place different emphases on various aspects of inner healing ministry. For many years, I have been helping churches in the Far East to manage mental health problems amongst their congregations. I have witnessed inner healing in practice. Deliverance from evil spirits is invariably part of their ministry. However, the same does not hold true in the churches of the West, where there is less acceptance of deliverance, despite belief in evil spirits still being common. Gargoyles intended to ward off evil spirits, still adorn cathedrals and churches, especially in Europe. Churches of Orthodox tradition even have specific rituals to deal with evil spirits.

There is an incident recorded in Matthew 16:23 where Peter's mind is apparently influenced by evil. The narrative begins with Jesus telling His disciples about His pending suffering, crucifixion and resurrection. Unhappy to hear this, Peter takes Jesus aside and rebukes Him. Jesus responds by saying, "Get behind me, Satan! You are a stumbling block to me; you do not have in mind the concerns of God, but merely human concerns." If evil spirits do exist, we need to consider that perhaps they can affect our minds as well.

UNDERSTANDING THE SPIRIT

As a Christian prayer minister and psychotherapist, I too have grappled with the issue of matters pertaining to both mental health and spirituality. Whilst many think these two subjects are antagonistic towards each other, in fact, they share a number of common features. Mental health affects the way we function, meaning it naturally has an impact on our interpersonal relationships and productivity in our communities. Likewise, spirituality—which is defined as a connection to something, someone, or some purpose bigger than ourselves—also affects the way we function. Spirituality involves finding meaning or purpose in life, and can thus result in positive emotions, thoughts and behaviours, and interpersonal relationships. Putting the two definitions side by side, examining them, and reflecting on them without bias, impresses upon us just how many similarities there are between the mental and the spiritual.

Many people who embrace spirituality believe that human beings consist of both physical and non-physical parts. Christians have the same belief, but their spirituality is rooted in the belief of a Creator God who is very personal and is deeply interested in their affairs, both physical and spiritual. For example, the book of Leviticus in the Old Testament of the Bible contains many teachings and instructions pertaining to both day-to-day physical health and spiritual rites and practices. Christian spirituality therefore is relational and far more personal than a belief in some unseen forces and influences. It is also consistent with the Genesis account of the creation of humans:

So, God created mankind in his own image, in the image of God he created them; male and female he created them.

— GENESIS 1:27

Then the Lord God formed a man from the dust of the ground and breathed into his nostrils the breath of life, and the man became a living being.

— GENESIS 2:7

God created humans in His own image as rational, emotional, volitional, and spiritual beings. *From the dust of the earth, man is created physical. From the breath of God, man is created spiritual.* This is consistent with the Hebraic concept that human beings are both earthly and spiritual. This belief that man consists of the physical and spiritual is known as bipartite man. Thus, the totality of our being includes both our physical and spiritual selves. That is why Moses, when urging us to love God with the totality of our being, says, "Love the Lord your God with all your heart and with all your soul and with all your strength" (Deuteronomy 6:5).

The Hebraic concept is that human beings consist of the physical, which is the body, and the non-physical, which is the real essence of a person, varyingly described as the heart, soul, or spirit. However, Greek thinking understands the non-physical as consisting of the soul *and* the spirit. Likewise, the Apostle Paul, being educated in Greek thinking, saw the non-physical part of a human as consisting of both soul and spirit. He writes in 1 Thessalonians 5:23:

> *May God himself, the God of peace, sanctify you through and through. May your whole **spirit, soul and body** be kept blameless at the coming of our Lord Jesus Christ.*

Thus, Christians who embrace Paul's teaching see humans as tri-partite beings.

The Greek word for spirit is *pneuma*, but it is from the Greek root word for soul—*psyche*—that we derive the words "psychology" and "psychiatry". Both disciplines relate to the study and treatment of the psyche which is defined as the mental structure of a person. It is the centre of our emotions, thoughts, and motivations. The psyche and the spirit are closely linked and even intertwined. The author of Hebrews writes:

> *For the word of God is alive and active. Sharper than any double-edged sword, it penetrates even to dividing soul and spirit, joints, and marrow; it judges the thoughts and attitudes of the heart.*
>
> — *HEBREWS 4:12*

It seems the spirit and psyche are so intertwined that one affects the other and vice versa. That is why the Apostle Paul states:

> *For who knows a person's thoughts except their own spirit within them? In the same way no one knows the thoughts of God except the Spirit of God.*
>
> — *1 CORINTHIANS 2:11*

He also ties the spiritual and the mental together in Romans 12:1 and 2:

Therefore, I urge you, brothers, and sisters, in view of God's mercy, to offer your bodies as a living sacrifice, holy and pleasing to God—this is your true and proper worship. Do not be conformed to the pattern of this world but be transformed by the renewing of your mind. Then you will be able to test and approve what God's will is—his good, pleasing, and perfect will.

I once had the privilege of journeying with a Christian pastor who sought me out for help, although he did not have any specific diagnosable mental health problems. Customary to my practice, I asked him during the first session why he had decided to see me. He replied, "For transformation of the mind."

I offered him psychotherapy, and during these sessions, he would bring up concerns he had in his life. I would then help him to understand his own motivations, desires, fears, emotions and thoughts. He had weekly therapy with me for two years. Frequently, he would bring the matters covered in our sessions into his personal devotional time. When his therapy journey came to an end, this pastor said he understood himself and his motivations better, which in turn improved his spiritual life. The transformation of our minds has a big impact on our spirituality.

MENTAL HEALTH AND CHRISTIAN SPIRITUALITY

During a Christian conference I attended some years ago, I met a Christian brother. As we spoke, he learnt I am a child, adolescent, and family psychiatrist. He soon remarked that the Bible is the best counselling book in the world, and I only needed to study the Word of God in order to be a good psychiatrist. His stated belief typifies a lot of Christians who have an antagonistic view of Christian spirituality, psychology and psychiatry. In my heart, I could not have disagreed with him more.

I have a reverence for the Word of God. I believe it to be infallible and inerrant. I also believe the disciplines of psychology and psychiatry have to do with the study of the abnormal mind and its treatment and healing. These disciplines provide a deeper understanding of human beings and what makes us tick, the reasons behind our mental health problems, and how we can successfully manage them or even heal them completely. However, that does not mean I accept everything I learn within those fields. Though there has been a great deal of advancement in neuroscience since the days of Sigmund Freud, Carl Jung and John Watson, and though psychiatrists and psychologists seek to be evidence-based in their therapeutics today, the human mind is infinitely complex. It sits well within the realm of the mysteries of God.

Further, I do not think the Bible itself claims to be a textbook on psychological treatment. Primarily it is a collection of books which describe and detail the relationship of God with His people—firstly the Jews and then the Gentiles. The Bible also details the relationships of human beings with one another. It has many passages which cover complex interpersonal dynamics. In the book of Genesis, we discover family feuds, sibling rivalry, family intrigue, jealousy, loyalty, and love. The Book of Job records the author's own struggle with mental health problems and his final triumph. The Wisdom Books are replete with good advice for stable mental health, while Jesus' teaching known as the Beatitudes is as much advice on good mental health as it is a path to Kingdom living. I believe that Christian spirituality has been under-explored as an approach to mental health problems such as anxiety and fear.

MY INNER HEALING JOURNEY

Some years ago, my wife started her own journey into inner healing, attending a weekend seminar on "Freedom from Fear" at a healing centre in Sydney. I was most sceptical of her choice, and I took it upon myself to go along and make sure that she was not exposed to any heresies. I remember sitting in a corner of the room, profusely taking notes and checking Bible verses in case they were taken out of context. That was the beginning of my interest in inner healing. The next three years saw me enrolled in their structured teaching programs. Since then, I have been on both the receiving and giving ends of prayer ministry, and I also have the privilege of playing an integral role in extending the ministry to Malaysia and the Far East.

Despite witnessing my wife's wonderful foray into this new world, my personal journey into inner healing only began around the same time I started bringing Christian spirituality into my psychiatric practice. It was therefore interesting to note that the patients who allowed the exploration of their Christian faith tended to fare better than those who kept their faith separate from their mental health problems. Around this time, other mental health practitioners also started bringing elements of spirituality into the disciplines of psychology and psychiatry. But not all of these spiritual aspects that are now included are compatible with the Christian faith.

As a prayer minister and a child, adolescent, and family psychiatrist, I have the tremendous privilege of journeying with my patients during a key period in their lives. I appreciate learning which practices can help in their mental health management and which practices don't. Seeing Christian patients in the context of their mental health problems helps me to really appreciate the role of Christian spirituality in their journey of healing. And I believe that this more open approach helps me to be a more effective therapist.

5

The Nature of Christian Spirituality

When I began my post-graduate study in child, adolescent, and family psychiatry, I had to complete fifty hours of infant observation, recording how the infant behaved in his environment and interacted with his parents and wider family. The emphasis on infant observation is based on the belief that our developmental history, early experiences, and the way we interact with our caregivers early in life, all affect our future emotional functioning and relationships. Early relationships are particularly important. They shape our emotional and psychological development, and all our early experiences of connecting with our caregivers ultimately contribute to building up the final blueprint in our minds. This blueprint then guides and influences how we approach and manage relationships throughout our life journey. Most of us follow the blueprint consciously or unconsciously until we encounter an emotional problem, experience a relationship difficulty, or develop a mental health issue. If at this point we seek help from a mental health professional such as a psychiatrist or a psychologist, they may help us understand how our early relationships shaped our psychological development towards relationships in general. We can then begin the process of altering our original blueprint by discarding unhelpful beliefs, strengthening more helpful beliefs, and even adopting new ones.

Changing an unhealthy internal model around relationships allows us to live differently from what we may have previously perceived as normal, when in fact it was unhelpful or untrue.

For me, Christian spirituality is also about relationship. It is not about connecting to an unknown higher power or achieving a higher principle. It is about our unique and personal relationship with the Creator of the universe, the originator of life and of all things. This relationship is as much tangible as it is spiritual. It is more than just a state of transcendental bliss—it is an awareness of that divine relationship within our daily, earthly lives.

CHRISTIAN SPIRITUALITY IS RELATIONAL

We don't live life in a vacuum devoid of relationship. I remember reading the book *Robinson Crusoe* by Daniel Defoe when I was in fifth grade. Robinson was stranded alone on a deserted island, where he had to learn to fend for himself and survive in a foreign environment. One day, he met a native whom he called Friday, and his life changed as a result. Finally, he had found a companion. Through Friday, Robinson learnt about the customs and culture of the indigenous people on the island. Despite their very different backgrounds, there was a true and strong connection between Robinson and Friday. As a young boy, I thought the relationship with Friday was the turning point in Robinson's life. He shifted to living life instead of merely surviving it.

Likewise, Christian spirituality is about directly relating with a knowable and lovable God. We may be knowledgeable in various principles, such as how to live without fear and anxiety, but we cannot love a set of life principles no matter how true they are. Christian spirituality only comes about when we have a deep sense of love and being loved—and these come through a deep and secure relationship with our Creator. In this world, within our frame of reference and experience, it is the same self-sacrificial and "agape" love as that of a mother towards her child. The deep love of a mother allows love to be so truly manifested in her child's life that the child can only love in return.

This is what it is to be human, for we are created to love and to be loved by our heavenly father. This is why Christian spirituality is relational at the core. It is about building a relationship as a child of God (John 1:12). The practices of meditation, reflection, prayer ministry, and reading the Word of God are but the means towards that end. Unfortunately for many Christians, meditation and reflection are a lost tradition and practice, as we tend to live life nowadays in a hectic and overly busy manner. Another reason these practices can fall to the wayside is the mistaken fear that any hint of meditation, reflection, or metaphysical activities are to be rejected as "new age" or non-Christian.

CHRISTIAN SPIRITUALITY IS DEVELOPMENTAL

The Christian faith not only proclaims the remarkable notion that God has called us to be His children, but it also states that God has a plan for each of us (Romans 8:28 and 29, Ephesians 2:8-10). The idea of God creating a personal plan for His children is a central theme in the Bible, and this idea is not too foreign when we consider the matter of parenting. Those who are in a long-term relationship and have children can perhaps resonate with this. We know that even before we have children, we talk with our partner about having a child. We imagine the gender and personality of the child, and what it might be like sharing life with this child. Then, we plan for that child. From the moment we know a new life has been conceived, our preoccupation is on the child inside the womb. The mother is aware of the movement of her child during the pregnancy, and both parents communicate with the child by touching and talking or singing. Then, after our child is born, we provide for, supervise, and guide them towards their potential in living out their own unique life.

Likewise, God has a plan for each one of us, and it is His pleasure to set out plans for His children. Viewed in this way, Christian spirituality is clearly developmental. Becoming a Christian is not just a matter of going to Heaven after this life; rather it is a matter of living our earthly life in such a way that we can achieve our true potential with all the gifts and talents

God has given us, whilst developing and nurturing our relationship with our heavenly father.

Let us examine the life of Abraham to further illustrate the point. Abraham is the father of faith for the three major religions in the world: Judaism, Christianity, and Islam. His life history is recorded in the book of Genesis chapters 11 to 25. These chapters track the migration of Abraham from his home country to a foreign land as he followed God's lead, (Genesis 11:26-32) and they also record his death (Genesis 25). Abraham was seventy-five years old when he left his birthplace (Genesis 12:4) and he died when he was one hundred and seventy-five years old (Genesis 25:7-8). During those one hundred years, God was "doing life" with Abraham in a very earthly sense, shaping and developing him to embrace the plan God had intended for him.

Abraham was not given a set of instructions or specific principles on how to cultivate his faith and live out his life according to God's plan. Instead, he learnt through real-life experiences and "seeing" the hand of God in his life. For example, twice he pretended that his wife Sarah was his sister, because of his fear that he would be killed by Pharaoh (Genesis 12) and later by Abimelech (Genesis 20). Both times, God intervened to save his life and preserve his relationship with his wife. God was also on hand in Abraham's family feud when Sarah could not get along with Hagar whom Abraham had taken as a second wife upon Sarah's initial encouragement (Genesis 21). Later on, Abraham had a deep and meaningful discussion with God about His plan for Sodom and Gomorrah (Genesis 19). Throughout these lived experiences, Abraham and God nurtured a real and intimate connection, and Abraham developed as a person to fulfil the plan God had for his life. He was even called a friend of God (James 2:23).

CHRISTIAN SPIRITUALITY IS ASPIRATIONAL

I believe the crux of inner healing is more than prayer ministry, identifying untruths, extending forgiveness, or in some cases experiencing deliverance from evil spirits. For me, these things are simply removing the roadblocks that impede our journey towards our final destiny. They are but the means to an end and not the end themselves. I think this is the weakness of the tripartite model which teaches that these healing steps are applied in order to remove the soul's control over our life so that the spirit can rise up. In my experience, the bipartite model is simpler and less confusing. To use a gardening example, it is like pulling out weeds so that a plant will flourish. But we don't stop at the weeding—we water and fertilise and do more weeding until the plant bears fruit. In a spiritual sense, our goal is a thriving relationship with God, inviting Him into our experience of joy and sadness, our dreams and passions, our tears and jubilation. In all our earthly experiences, whether we suffer with mental health problems or not, we remain aware that He is always with us—our heavenly father, present, intimately connected with us, and always dependable.

If I may use an earthly example to drive home the point, let me share my own experience as the child of my parents and as a parent to my own children. As a child, I knew that in all circumstances there would be a meal for me at home, a comfortable bed for me to sleep on, and that I would be safe and secure in my own home. I did not fear that my parents would try to extract rent from me, lease out my room or throw my belongings out onto the front lawn—I knew they would always provide stability and support. As a parent myself, I attempt to be there for my children in all circumstances as well. I strive to be reliable, dependable, and consistent, just as God, our heavenly father is always there for us.

The famous paediatrician and psychoanalyst, Donald Winnicott, once said, "There is no such thing as a baby."[10] He meant we cannot consider a baby as separate from its caregiver—usually the mother. The baby is inseparable from the mother, and on its own, it would cease to exist. With the same sentiment and conviction, I say, "There is no such thing as a Christian." We cannot consider a Christian without God. Our relationship with God is the basis of our spiritual and mental health! Inner healing centred on Christian spirituality is part of discovering the abundant life Jesus spoke over us and

---

10 Winnicott, D. W., *The maturational processes and the facilitating environment: Studies in the theory of emotional development.* International Universities Press, 1965.

becoming all that we are created to be. Despite our struggles, God sees our potential and our capacity, and He works within us to bring to completion the plan He has for us (Philippians 2:13). His desire is to bring to fruition our ultimate transformation in a state of glory (Romans 8:28-30).

I do believe we cannot express our humanity without our spirituality because the true essence of oneself is within our spirituality. This is why I have concluded that to be human is to be spiritual. I consider that the biopsychosocial approach to mental health treatment *without* the consideration of spirituality is incomplete. The theories of the mind and the various schools of psychotherapies help me to understand the interpersonal and intrapersonal dynamics and the reasons behind mental health problems themselves. But for many patients, including Christians, the spirituality aspect is lacking.

Most mental health problems originate from failed relationships—both past and present—resulting in deep feelings of fear, anxiety, insecurity, rejection, and abandonment. Christian spirituality provides another dimension to understand and to help those who suffer from mental health problems. These problems have robbed many Christians of realising their true potential in life, and they can only be dealt with in partnership with our Father God who is the creator of human relationships (Ephesians 3:14-15).

CASE STUDIES

Allow me to return to the two cases I shared with you in Chapter 3. There we looked at the biopsychosocial factors that contributed to their mental health struggles. Now let's hone in on the spiritual component.

Robert Smith

Robert Smith is the fifty-five-year-old Christian gentleman who was referred to me by his general practitioner for treatment of his obsessive compulsive disorder characterised by intrusive sexual thoughts and images. I treated Robert with a biopsychosocial approach, including the use of medication, psychotherapy, and social support. He made a good but incomplete recovery from his OCD, and I decided to look deeper into his condition. With his permission, I invited his wife to join one of my sessions with Robert to obtain a corroborative history from her, as is my usual practice. Whenever a patient is not making as straightforward progress as anticipated, I will ask permission to interview significant family members to gain a wider perspective on the patient's struggles. It is not uncommon to uncover new information this way, which had previously been omitted by the patient—either knowingly or unknowingly.

With third-person insight from his wife, I learned that, after thirty years of teaching, Robert was experiencing burnout and found he had decreased motivation in his teaching job. He was stressed and bored, and he turned to internet pornography for emotional comfort. Soon he began experiencing intrusive sexual thoughts and images, resulting in him feeling shame and fear. Robert tried to stop accessing pornography sites but did not succeed for long. Like many who are addicted to various substances, he went through cycles of abstinence and relapse. The intrusive images and thoughts became stronger, and he became so concerned that he would act out the sexual thoughts in his mind, that he quit his teaching career. But Robert's shame and guilt were not assuaged, and his change of profession did little to reduce the intensity of his obsessive compulsive symptoms.

When his attempt at a printing business failed, Robert felt even more guilt over now squandering his brother's money. He decided he had sinned greatly and therefore deserved punishment, and he began lying on the cold concrete floor at night to punish himself for his wrongdoings. The treatment I had offered of medication combined with psychological therapy and social support, did help Robert to see that his fear of acting out obsessive thoughts and images was irrational. But unfortunately, it did little to address his innate feelings of guilt and shame.

With this deeper insight into his struggles, I brought the spiritual dimension of grace, hope, and God's love into my therapy sessions with Robert. I helped him to understand that his obsessive compulsive disorder was a result of an unmet need—emotional comfort—which he had tried to address through internet pornography. Unfortunately, his attempted solution to his problem had become a new problem in and of itself. When Robert then quit his job and started a new business only to fail, it further exacerbated his guilt and shame. But now, with grace in the picture, I helped Robert to see that his compulsive behaviour of self-punishment, such as lying on a cold concrete floor, would not resolve anything and would only allow the cycle of shame and guilt to continue unimpeded.

Instead of going down the track of examining the rationality behind Robert's self-flagellation, I brought in the Christian spiritual dimension of grace. This resonated with him, and we explored the biblical teaching on law and grace (Romans chapters 6 to 8). Previously, Robert had understood the issue of legalism versus grace in an intellectual way. Now, he had to embrace it in a personal, life-changing way. It was a case of intellectual insight versus spiritual insight. Intellectual insight *enriches* our mind, and spiritual insight *transforms* our mind. Psychiatry imparts intellectual insight, but it is spirituality that imparts spiritual insight. This is why I affirm that spirituality is an important part of mental health treatment and healing.

Now, Robert had to make a spiritual choice—would he embrace legalism or grace? In order to take grace on board personally, he needed to accept that his failures could not be addressed by self-condemnation or self-punishment. Rather, he would have to make the radical decision to implement actual change, in order to turn his life towards a different direction. As his psychiatrist, I could not do this for Robert. I could guide him into the spiritual dimension to facilitate change, but taking the next step would be up to him. It was Robert who therefore made the important shift in his understanding, accepting that his persistence in embracing shame and guilt was a wilful attempt to nullify the grace of God. He decided to ask God for forgiveness for what he saw as a form of pride, and in so doing, he was also able to forgive himself for his addiction to internet pornography and his business failure.

Robert eventually found freedom of both mind and spirit. He recovered fully from his obsessive compulsive disorder, and he no longer feels guilt and shame about himself. Interestingly, he has even found enough motivation to return to casual teaching, finding new enjoyment in his old profession. To this day, he remains well with robust mental health.

Teresa Khoo

Teresa is the thirty-six-year-old Christian lady who was referred to me with an obsessive compulsive disorder characterised by intrusive images and thoughts of stabbing someone with a knife. Teresa's disorder was linked to her childhood trauma of domestic violence perpetrated by her father. A significant event that etched the trauma further into her psyche happened when she was just eight years old; her father threatened her mother with a knife. That was the last time that Teresa saw her father. Her mother took both daughters and fled with them to their grandparents' house, but Teresa only found out some years later that her father had taken his own life not long after their escape. She felt terribly guilty. She had often wished her father dead, and she couldn't shake the sense that her death wish for her father had led to his demise. Treatment with medication and psychological therapy, including exploring her relationship with her late father and her forgiveness of herself for wishing him dead, did not achieve a complete recovery.

Once again I delved in deeper, bringing the spiritual dimension into Teresa's treatment. Many Christians who suffer a traumatic relationship with their earthly father are more likely to have a distant spiritual relationship with God the Father. Some may even have a lack of trust in God, and I soon found out that Teresa did indeed find it difficult to feel close to God. She often doubted God would keep His promises, and she felt that some of her answered prayers were mere coincidences.

Together, Teresa and I explored her Christian belief and foundation. We referred to Bible verses that speak of the faithfulness of God such as Lamentations 3:22-23, and these helped prepare her to move on to a spiritual exercise. For this exercise, I had her recall one traumatic incident from her past when she would have wished her father dead. I then asked her to invite God—who is timeless and eternal—into that experience. I allowed

Teresa the space to interact with God in this memory, and she found herself holding a great sense of peace within that experience. She sensed that God understood her genuine fear and would therefore not hold her accountable for her death wish towards her father.

That session set Teresa on a new trajectory towards recovery. She began to see God's faithfulness in the little and big things in her life. One day, fully confident of her recovery, she decided that the obsessive compulsive disorder had no grip over her life, and she asked to come off her medication. As I pen her story, she has not experienced another relapse since.

My therapeutic journey with Teresa illustrates the importance of the therapeutic space—the environment and relationship between a therapist and a patient during therapy. The therapeutic space is a safe and confidential place where we can discuss our feelings, thoughts and problems without fear of judgment. It is not a physical space but is relational in nature. When I further apply a spiritual dimension to a session, I prefer to use my own term of *Spiritual Space*. For Christians, the therapeutic space is a space of three, namely my patient, myself, and God. I do nothing to create this space, except welcoming a state of stillness in my spirit in anticipation of God's work. I behave more as an observer and a facilitator, with the main focus on redirecting whatever happens in the *Spiritual Space* back to the relationship between my patients and God. I often use words or examples in the Scriptures, for example in the case of Teresa, where I drew her attention to the fact that God has a special heart for the fatherless and the fearful.

I believe our spirituality has a great impact on our psychological and mental life whether we are aware of it or not. I have seen firsthand how adding a spiritual dimension to the biopsychosocial approach helps to bring about a greater understanding of mental health problems and the journey towards healing. As Robert and Teresa both discovered, it will change us in a profound way.

6

Anxiety: A Spiritual Biopsychosocial Perspective

Fear and anxiety are two common mental health problems that share certain characteristics. Both are associated with an increase in the hormone called adrenaline which causes the well-known fight-flight response in the body. However, fear is normally an intense and immediate emotional response to an actual threat or danger. The body thus responds naturally with an increased output of adrenaline to confront or flee the dangerous or threatening trigger. The person gripped by fear experiences increased heart rate, sweating, muscle tension, and a faster respiratory rate with a sense of hyper-alertness. The emotional and physiological responses of fear are time-limited and short-lived, with the person returning to a state of calm once the threat or danger is over. Anxiety, on the other hand, is usually associated with generalised emotional distress, despite the elements of threat or danger often being absent. Anxiety's trigger is less specific than that of fear, and it can be associated with multiple stressors. It tends to be more prolonged and can even be chronic. People who suffer from anxiety commonly experience sleep disturbance, increased muscle tension, restlessness, an inability to relax, and concentration problems.

TYPES OF ANXIETY DISORDERS

Research shows that at any one time, 20-25% of the population suffers from a diagnosable anxiety problem. There are many different types of anxiety disorders, but the six most common which I see in my practice are:

Phobia: an irrational and excessive fear of an object or situation. Some common phobias are the fear of heights, a marketplace (agoraphobia), enclosed spaces (claustrophobia), being alone, social situations, illness, animals, insects, etc.

Generalised anxiety disorder: excessive worry or anxiety that is out of proportion to the circumstance or situation associated with our daily activities.

Separation anxiety disorder: an inability to separate and individuate from significant others. This commonly occurs in those with an insecure and anxious attachment to their significant others. This disorder may manifest as school refusal in children and adolescents.

Obsessive compulsive disorder: intrusive thoughts, urges, or images that produce fear, worry, or feelings of distress and uneasiness, often causing the person to perform repetitive, ritualistic behaviour to reduce the distressing and anxious feelings.

Some common obsessions are the fear of dirt, disease, destruction, decay, and death, with common ritualistic behaviours including compulsive cleaning, counting, and checking.

Panic disorder: unexpected, spontaneous, and recurrent panic attacks. The person will fear future attacks and is likely to avoid situations or places associated with past panic attacks.

Social anxiety disorder: excessive anxiety or fear of attending social situations or events. The person is concerned that he or she might behave in such a way that would invite negative feedback or criticism from others. Often, avoidance of the social situation or event altogether is preferred, irrespective of their importance. The degree of social anxiety may be more pronounced when the social situation or event is less familiar.

Existential anxiety: living with a general sense of dread and foreboding. Most of the time, the person also experiences a feeling of stress. These people often present with a diagnosis of generalised anxiety disorder. This is because there is an absence of specific worries in existential anxiety, as life itself is the source of anxiety.

People who experience early attachment problems and trauma with a sense of non-belonging, are particularly vulnerable to developing existential anxiety. Recently, we have seen a rise in existential anxiety, particularly amongst the old and young, due to the Covid pandemic, issues of global warming, and wars and rumours of wars. Existential anxiety is experienced by many, though as yet it is not included in the standard *International Classification of Diseases*[11] or the *Diagnostic and Statistical Manual of Mental Disorder*[12].

THE ROLE OF GENETICS

As mentioned, anxious people invariably struggle with feelings of uncertainty and insecurity. Anxiety has a genetic origin in that it can run in the same family, and anxious adults tend to have an early life history of insecure or anxious attachments. This results in a heightened sense of alertness, and the person becomes sensitised to perceived or real rejection, making them vulnerable towards developing social anxiety disorder. People who experience childhood trauma usually become hypervigilant and hyperalert individuals who are constantly restless. They have great difficulty in being relaxed and calm, and they tend to develop one or more anxiety disorders such as generalised anxiety disorder and social anxiety disorder. Children with a prominent history of rejection and abandonment are also more likely to develop anxiety problems. Rejection and abandonment deeply wound a person's psyche and spirit, with the person becoming less psychologically resilient and robust, and more likely to succumb to anxiety when confronted with stress.

---

11 At the time of writing, the International Classification of Diseases is in its 11th Edition (ICD 11)
12 At the time of writing, this publication is in its 5th Edition (DSM V)

CASE STUDY

I'd like to share the case of a particular patient whom I shall call James Yeomans[13].

James Yeomans (Obsessive Compulsive Disorder)

James is a thirty-five-year-old business executive who is very successful in his work. He is well-known amongst his peers, and he is a Christian who is actively engaged in his local church. James was referred to me because of his persistent anxiety that he was not performing well in his job, despite his relative success. To compensate for his persistent doubts, he developed the compulsive behaviour of overly checking his work for mistakes. I diagnosed obsessive compulsive disorder and offered to treat James with medication and counselling.

James told me that his compulsive checking began shortly after the sudden death of his father who suffered a heart attack. James was so stressed and upset by this unexpected loss that he could not concentrate at work. One day, he made a severe financial mistake which would have caused the company untold loss had he not discovered his error in good time. He was able to correct the mistake before it became a problem, but since then he had struggled with the persistent fear that he would make another mistake if he did not spend enough time checking.

Outside of this incident, James still described himself as a meticulous person who regularly checks tasks so that he does not make mistakes. This trait of thoroughness was "inherited" from his father who had taught him that mistakes can be costly. James remembers his father being a very methodical person who developed specific systems for various tasks. As a child, his father not only taught him exactly how to do things but also that he must not deviate from those ways. James had to stack dishes in the dishwasher in a certain way to maximise space. Tools had to be returned to the correct place in the tool shed, otherwise his father would be upset. His school bag had to be packed the night before and then checked the next morning when

---

13 Not his real name

he got out of bed. Once, James accidentally lost his lunchbox at school. His father refused to pack his lunch for the rest of the week to teach him a lesson in being more careful.

James described his father as a rather stern and distant person. "I tried to be close to him," he told me, but he did not remember sharing many fun times with his father. His mother was a warm person who compensated for his father's harshness, but for James, life was a series of strict coaching lessons from his father. Still, James admired his father for being a hard-working person with a strong work ethic. After high school, James did not know what university course to study. His father advised him to study commerce because of the job security, but James thought perhaps he should follow in his father's footsteps and become a banker.

Based on his history, I formulated that James has always been an anxious person with obsessional tendencies. He also had an anxious attachment with his father whom he idealised, to the extent that he patterned his own life after his father's in an effort to please him. James was not given an opportunity to develop the relationship between father and son, and whatever tenuous connection he had with his father was prematurely terminated by the latter's sudden death. I thought James might have a myriad of emotions including sadness, disappointment, and anger. However, he had pushed the negative emotions out of his consciousness, instead expressing them through obsessive compulsive disorder.

Through counselling, I led James to explore his relationship with his father—from James' early childhood to the time of his father's death. Initially, James spoke of how much his father had loved him, despite having limited memories of meaningful time spent together. But as he gained trust in me, James more openly began to express disappointment. He felt his father had been selfish and inconsiderate. As he allowed himself permission to talk about his father freely, his grief soon turned to anger and then to rage towards his father. He lamented bitterly about his father's lack of love and compassion towards him. James resented that he had worked so hard to win his father's heart, but to no avail.

Through the safety of our therapeutic forum, James was able to see that he has had an anxiety problem all his life. He had used his perfectionism as a coping mechanism for his anxiety and as a way to potentially win his father's love. Now he could see that the more perfectionistic he became, the more anxious he became too—he kept missing the mark. James also came to realise that, as a Christian, he had approached his relationship with Father God in the same way. He had viewed Father God as a hard taskmaster whose standards he would never reach. Deep in his spirit and psyche, James had known little of the grace of God.

James' bereavement had brought him to a crisis regarding his Christian belief about Father God and his own spiritual sonship. He could see that his spiritual life was full of striving to gain the approval of Father God, whilst also believing he could never fully earn His love. When he finally allowed himself to embrace the grace of Father God in all its fullness, James was able to let go of his grief, anger, and pain. He was also able to let go of the idealised father image that he had internalised in his heart, and he discovered a new dimension in his own identity of being a son of God. James gained newfound freedom, and since then his life has become much less rigid. His obsessive compulsive disorder lost its grip on his life, and he even stopped taking his medication. He continued his psychotherapy with me for another year before being discharged from my care. To this day, James embraces the grace and love that God has towards him, without believing he has to earn it.

ANXIETY AND OUT-OF-HOME (FOSTER) CARE

A few years ago, the Lord impressed upon me the idea of opening my appointment book to out-of-home care (or, foster care) young people. These young people do not live with their biological family and are considered wards of the state (though they are no longer referred to in this way) under the guardianship of the state represented by the minister of health. Like many child, adolescent and family psychiatrists, I used to avoid taking on such cases because they are a very difficult group of patients to treat. These children and youth usually present with multiple mental health problems, particularly anxiety disorders. They also tend to have various neurodevelopmental disorders such as attention deficit hyperactivity disorder and learning problems. However, the main frustration for me is the lack of permanence in the foster care system.

When I stepped in as a therapist for this group of young people, I learnt they often lack a sense of belonging which further gives rise to deep insecurities about themselves and uncertainty about the future. The feeling of not belonging is an existential issue that cannot be overcome with medication, relaxation, and guided imagery. An inner unrest sits buried within the person, and life becomes a state of perpetual angst accompanied by a sense of unreality. Often, they resort to self-harm, with the pain and the sight of blood confirming to themselves that there is still life within them. They also report that medicine numbs their mind and emotions, further asserting their sense of an inner void and nothingness—and this is unbearable.

CASE STUDY

I have the privilege of being the child and adolescent psychiatrist for two sisters who I will identify as Emily and Danielle[14]. They are currently fostered together within the same family, where they have been for about four years now. Emily was thirteen and Danielle was eight when the foster program first integrated them into this family. Their foster parents are an older couple whose adult children have left home, and who have a heart to help disadvantaged young people. Previous to these foster parents, Emily and Danielle had been living with another couple for two years. However, the placement broke down when it was discovered that this couple did not treat Emily and Danielle well. The sisters were frequently sent to their room without meals as punishment for minor misdemeanours or alleged bad behaviour. There were also allegations of the couple physically abusing the girls.

Even before entering this home, Emily and Danielle had suffered an impoverished childhood, replete with emotional abuse and physical neglect.

---

14 Not their real names

Their biological parents have a history of drug and alcohol abuse and criminal records, and their home was frequented by people purchasing drugs from their parents. The girls' father was in and out of jail for drug peddling, theft, and assaults. Worse, their mother was in jail for child abuse after her actions resulted in the death of their younger sister. Their mother had allegedly thrown the two-year-old against the wall, citing bad behaviour. Both Emily and Danielle were eyewitnesses to the incident. At the time, they were nine and four respectively. The girls were both placed in foster care soon after their mother went to jail.

Danielle Adam (Extreme anxiety and ADHD)

Let's start with Danielle, who was referred to me when she was just eight years old. What stood out to me when I first met Danielle was her extreme anxiety, timidity, restlessness, and limited ability to relate. She was not performing well academically at school, her peer relationships were poor, and she needed to be constantly directed by the teacher due to her lack of initiative. At home with their foster parents, Danielle was a model child. Her foster mother observed that the little girl was constantly eager to please—as if she was fearful of making a mistake. Later, I found out that when Danielle was being "disciplined" by her previous foster parents, she often did not even know what she had done wrong. She would frequently be sent to her room without meals or else grounded indoors and not allowed to play outside.

I began treating Danielle with medication for her extreme anxiety. I also diagnosed her with attention deficit hyperactivity disorder and treated her with a psychostimulant medication. Due to her relative lack of verbal ability, I offered her play therapy instead of talking therapy. The first picture she drew for me was of herself, and she placed her figure in the lower corner of the page with blobs of black in the background. The next picture was of her family. Danielle drew herself and her older sister Emily—who appeared much larger than Danielle—and a little baby tucked in the upper right corner of the page. I interpreted her drawings as depicting her insignificant self, the absence of parental figures, and her dead little sister in heaven. Later, I found out that the previous foster parents had often locked Danielle in a closet. This explained the blobs of black in her first drawing.

Through regular therapy and her newly nurturing foster environment, Danielle improved slowly. Play therapy was slowly replaced with talking therapy, and she began to speak more about herself as I helped her to explore her inner world. Daniel was soon talking about her wishes, desires, and hopes. She started to make friends at school, and she took part in extracurricular activities such as arts and dancing which she truly enjoyed. She also began to see herself as an integral part of her foster family whom she wishes to stay with as long as possible, even after she turns eighteen.

Danielle's grades continued to improve at school. I had first seen her when she was in Year 3 and struggling, but by the time she was in Year 6 she had reached an average level in most of her grades. She attempted to run for school captain, and though she did not make it, she managed to become the house captain instead. Danielle began looking forward to high school with a degree of anxiety which I considered normal. She genuinely enjoyed school, and she dared to share with me her hope of becoming a teacher. She also talked about joining the youth group at church as she had eventually followed her foster mother to church and found it to be a safe and welcoming place.

Danielle's transition into high school was essentially uneventful. Since then, I have continued to see her, albeit less frequently. She is still taking medication because she still feels stressed from time to time. Her foster mother tells me that Danielle can be quite harsh on herself in terms of doing the right thing. She can easily feel guilty if she perceives that she has done something wrong, but she is feeling more secure in her relationship with her foster parents. She talks freely about her Christian faith in a real and tangible way, and she continues to improve. I feel confident about Danielle's prognosis and ongoing life.

Emily Adam (Anxiety, ADHD)

Emily, Danielle's older sister, was thirteen years old when she was referred to me. A teenager in Year 7, she presented quite differently from her younger sister. Whilst Danielle was a severely anxious young lady, Emily was angry. She was reluctant to see me and was not forthcoming in her communication. She declared it a waste of her precious time to repeat her story to yet another doctor, and she was sceptical of my ability to actually help her. But underlying her angry demeanour, Emily's inner anxiety was palpable. Despite her present loving foster home, she still carried anxiety about her previous foster placement and the possibility that in her future she may be uprooted again.

I began by prescribing medication for her anxiety. Emily was also diagnosed with attention deficit hyperactivity disorder by her paediatrician, and thus far had been treated with a psychostimulant medication which I decided to continue. As a result of her anxiety problems and attention deficit hyperactivity disorder, Emily was restless and inattentive. She was not engaging with her teachers at school, and she sat at the bottom 25% of her grade. Her peer relationships were also poor, as she was defensive and aggressive, and her peers were fearful of her. She did not affiliate with any particular peer group but drifted from group to group aimlessly.

Emily was equally difficult to engage with in counselling. I worked hard to establish a rapport with her, but it took one year of regular counselling before I finally broke through to her. Initially, our sessions had been quite short. But after one year, Emily managed to remain in my room for the full session. That being said, Emily is still greatly lacking in the ability to reflect. She has a tendency to project blame onto others, and her ability to test reality remains poor, even after years of therapy.

Emily's life is characterised by interpersonal crises. At school, there are frequent arguments with teachers, failure to complete classwork, truanting, and absence from school for no reason. At home, she is oppositional and argumentative. She has great difficulty fitting in, and she has even run away from home without cause. Emily has often indicated she does not wish to remain in her foster home—but she always returns after disappearing for a few days. Two years ago, Emily began to cut herself. She also scratched and picked at her skin. During one session with me, she told me that the pain inflicted by the self-harm makes her feel alive. Otherwise, she feels that she has nothing inside her at all.

Emily told me she wants to be a tough person so that other people will not pick on her. Unlike her sister, Danielle, she has no time for God. She tends to be a loner, and she frequently withdraws herself from family activities including family vacations. She seems to have a limited ability to empathise, and on numerous occasions she has abused her foster mother's credit cards by purchasing things online. Though she has verbally expressed remorse, she shows no behavioural change. Emily is also unable to form long-term relationships because she believes that people generally cannot be trusted. She is marginally less anxious than when I first met her, however she remains purposeless in her life. There is still an inner void and an emptiness in the depths of her psyche and spirit.

Neither Emily nor Danielle have openly discussed their early trauma with me. But Danielle seems to have responded well to the secure relationship offered by their new foster family. She has managed to overcome some of her early trauma, rejection, abandonment, and neglect. She has also found a meaningful relationship with God. Unfortunately, Emily has failed to find healing to the same extent as Danielle. No doubt, she was exposed to the trauma a lot longer than her sister who is four years younger. I also wonder if Emily had other traumas perpetrated against her, that she has consciously or unconsciously repressed. I do believe that, deep inside, Emily is afraid to change. Change can be painful and difficult. It brings unknown consequences—an automatic deterrent for a trauma survivor. For many, it is simply easier to remain in pain. Paradoxically, it is the fear of change that holds us back from a better future.

7

Fear: A Spiritual Biopsychosocial Perspective

Fear is a very common human experience. At some point in our lives, all of us will experience some type of fear. An emotion triggered by the anticipation of threat or danger, fear is a necessary response to ensure our survival in response to the threat. Most fears are the result of previous trauma. For example, a person may develop a fear of dogs after being bitten by one. Another person who suffers from agoraphobia—the fear of being in situations or places where escape or help may not be readily available— might have suffered from panic attacks in the past. Typically, when a person suffers a panic attack, they feel helpless and desperate to escape the situation. Such a person would end up avoiding crowded places, public transportation, open spaces, or places they feel could become a trap, such as elevators and tunnels. The person will be fearful of getting another panic attack, and would therefore avoid places likely to induce that sort of fear.

Some fears—fear of predators, fear of heights, fear of darkness, fear of aloneness—are so common they are universally experienced by human beings, and have been throughout the ages. These fears are most obvious in our early childhood, when there is no history of trauma. Carl Jung, a prominent Swiss psychiatrist and psychoanalyst in the 20th Century, observed that there are dreams, imageries, beliefs, and fears common to many races—even though there is no evidence of any direct sharing of knowledge and experience. This led Jung to postulate the existence of the "collective unconscious" which is like a hidden storehouse of human experiences that affects our emotions, thoughts, and behaviours. The fear of darkness and of being alone are deeply rooted in our collective unconscious. Evolution theorists explain that these fears helped in the survival of our ancestors and were selected to ensure the survival of our species. Animal studies further show that fear can be transmitted generationally. Parent rats which learn to fear previously non-threatening experiences in the research laboratory, produce offspring that show the same fearful response—despite these offspring never being subjected to the same experiment.

THE ORIGIN OF FEAR

In the Bible, the book of Genesis records the beginning of human life on earth as we know it. It is the beginning of human history. Genesis chapters 1 and 2 not only describe the creation of life by God, but also the creation of relationships—between God and our forebears, and between our forebears themselves, Adam and Eve. The relationship between God and our forebears was characterised by secure connection, communication, and fellowship. It is the prototypic secure attachment between parent and child. God provides the security, supervision, protection, and provision for Adam and Eve to grow and subdue the environment in which they live. They function optimally in terms of their self-management, relationship with each other, and the management of their environment. In this way, God is the First Parent of humankind who provides a secure attachment for us.

Secure attachment is the antithesis of fear, generating a sense of acceptance, belonging and love. When there is love, there is no fear (1 John 4:18). When there is love, there is no rejection (1 John 3:1). Allow me to use our earthly life experience to understand the narrative in Genesis. When we experience a deep sense of attachment with our parents, we naturally feel a part of the family. We feel loved and accepted. We are confident. Children who are secure are more likely to explore their environment because they know their parents are always there for them. The child is never out of the awareness of the parents and therefore has no fear. This "invisible tie" connects the child to the parents with dependability and safety. Out of this sense of security, the child's experience is that the parents regard their child to be an important and valued person, which further grows that child's sense of significance. Such is the experience of Adam and Eve as described in Genesis 1 and 2.

When Adam and Eve ignored God's instruction, their response was immediate. Their confidence in their secure attachment to their Father was shaken, and fear set in. We read in Genesis 3:8-10:

> *Then the man and his wife heard the sound of the Lord God as he was walking in the garden in the cool of the day, and they hid from the Lord God among the trees of the garden. But the Lord God called to the man, "Where are you?" He answered, "I heard you in the garden, and I was afraid because I was naked; so I hid."*

The sound of the footsteps of God, which previously had brought the kind of joy and anticipation a child would feel towards a loving parent's approach, now brought fear instead. God came to reach out to them, but Adam and Eve had already internalised a sense of foreboding and dread. In response, they decided to hide from God. Remembering the warning of God that "you must not eat from the tree of the knowledge of good and evil, for when you eat from it, you will certainly die" (Genesis 2:17), shame and fear set in, and their response was to pull away from God.

Let us put ourselves in Adam and Eve's shoes. The experience of death was totally foreign to them. How can a person fully comprehend something of which they have no prior experience? And yet the character of God had remained unchanged. He sought them out—not to punish them, but to restore and reassure them.

God remained near, but from that time on, Adam and Eve fundamentally felt separated from God. The trauma to them was so great that their fear became primal. To this day, fear remains a universal human experience. All fears fall into one of the three primal categories:

- Fear of death. Fear of predators, heights, enclosed spaces, sicknesses, flying, and darkness are ultimately different manifestations of the fear of death.
- Fear of abandonment or rejection, which also includes the fear of separation.
- Fear of being insignificant. Fear of failure and the loss of autonomy are manifestations of the fear of insignificance.

Unlike God, no human parent can provide us with a perfectly secure sense of attachment. This is why we, as humans, are likely to suffer from one or more of these primal fears. For those of us who experience early separation in life—major disruptions to secure attachment, rejection, neglect, or abuse—it is all the more likely that fear will become a pervasive feature in our lives.

JACOB, THE PATRIARCH (A BIBLICAL STUDY)

The Bible says, "All Scripture is God-breathed and is useful for teaching, rebuking, correcting and training in righteousness so that the servant of God may be thoroughly equipped for every good work" (2 Timothy 3:16-17). It also contains the narratives of men and women of faith, without embellishing their good deeds or minimising their weaknesses, so that we can learn from them (Hebrews 11). Of the many different characters in the book of Genesis, I find Jacob to be the most interesting from a psychiatric perspective. He proves a very colourful character from whom we can learn about fear and how to overcome it.

Competition Breeds Fear of Missing Out (Genesis 25:21-26)

Jacob was born to Rebekah and Isaac, who had previously been childless for a long time. Rebekah finally became pregnant after her husband Isaac prayed to God. She was blessed with a twin pregnancy, but during her pregnancy, there was unrest in her womb. The twins inside her were jostling with each other as though in a state of constant strife and competition. Their beginnings inside the womb set the tone for their interaction and relationship later in life. When the time of delivery came, Esau was the firstborn son. But Jacob, though second in order, was not being left behind—he was born still holding fast to his brother Esau's heel. In a race, when there is no clear physical separation between two competing bodies, one can argue that both came first equally. In Hebrew, Jacob's name means "the supplanter", "one who seizes" and "grabs by the heel". From birth, Jacob behaved as though he feared missing out and being insignificant. This fear of missing out can often motivate us to act in ways that seem ruthless and unethical. Under the influence of fear, our rationality often takes a back seat, and we may behave in ways that we come to regret after the event.

Favouritism Leads to Fear of Insignificance (Genesis 25:27-34)

In Jacob's family, his parents each showed partiality towards their respective favourite son. Rebekah loved Jacob, while Isaac loved Esau. Jacob most probably did not have a secure attachment to his father Isaac, and his insecurity in this relationship would have heightened his fear of insignificance. He was fully aware of what he would miss by not being the first-born son. I opine that Jacob would have been quite preoccupied with how he had only marginally missed out on this birthright. The spontaneity with which he bargained with Esau for the birthright with a mere bowl of stew betrayed his eagerness. He leapt at the opportunity to seize what could have been his. It was Esau's despising of his own birthright which allowed Jacob to gain the upper hand, and if the elder brother had not been so carnal, perhaps Jacob would not have succeeded. As it was, Jacob's insecurity about his father's love, and his fear of insignificance, drove him to steal the birthright from Esau. To be assured of our worth and significance is a basic human need. Striving for power, fame and wealth is often the outworking of this unmet desire for significance. This is why many adolescents begin modelling their lives around "celebrities" whose lives they perceive as embodying significance. But a true sense of significance can only come from within our inner being.

Giving In to Our Fear Leads Us to Deception (Genesis 27:1-30)

When Isaac was old and his eyesight had become poor, he asked Esau to hunt some wild game for him to eat so that he could bless Esau before he died. Rebekah prompted Jacob to disguise himself as Esau so that Isaac's blessings would go to him instead. Despite having tricked his brother into handing over the birthright, Jacob was reluctant to deceive his father. He feared invoking a curse upon himself due to the deception. But Rebekah's rampant love for Jacob prompted her to accept the curse on Jacob's behalf. There was no restraint in her love towards her favourite son. Her belief in his worth and her willingness to take this action encouraged Jacob to collude with Rebekah.

Perceiving that his father loved him less, Jacob decided the only way to get a blessing was by deceit. His insecure attachment to Isaac and his fear of missing out on his father's blessings meant that he was willing to face any cost. Jacob was convinced that his life would become significant once he was the recipient of his father's blessings. As father and son sat on the threshold of this momentous event, Isaac twice expressed doubt that he was dealing with Esau. On both occasions, Jacob reassured Isaac that he was indeed Esau, the eldest son. Jacob's need for his father's love and his desperation to feel secure and significant in his father's eyes, were so great that he lied to his father at this most sacred moment. And so it was that Jacob obtained Isaac's blessings, reserved for the firstborn son, by deception.

Fear of The Unknown and Death (Genesis 27:41-45, 28:1-5)

When he learned that he had been deceived by Jacob, Esau vowed to kill his younger brother as soon as their father passed away. Jacob's insecurity and his fear of insignificance were now replaced by the very real fear of death. Nevertheless, Isaac loved both his sons. Although he sent Jacob away, he did so with kindness, and with the good advice to not marry a Canaanite woman. Isaac also pronounced upon Jacob the Abrahamic blessings, essentially making him the rightful heir to what God had promised his grandfather Abraham.

It's very probable that, in Isaac's spirit, Jacob was, in fact, the chosen one. Jacob too, desiring his father's blessing, obeyed his father's warning about choosing the right woman. This was a strength of Jacob's character. He valued his father's blessing so highly that he would not do anything to jeopardise this gift. This character strength was not present in Esau, who had carelessly tossed aside his birthright and went on to marry into the very clan his father had requested his sons avoid.

God Is There When We Are at the Depths of
Our Fear (Genesis 28:10-22)

Jacob was at a very low point in his life when he fled from Esau. He'd had to leave his parents and his community behind, and he took himself to an unfamiliar place to escape from his angry brother. His future was filled with uncertainty, and his level of fear must have been sky-high. Did he think all the scheming and plotting was not worth it? Was he regretful and remorseful about what he had done to his brother and father? It was in this depressive slump in his life that God met with Jacob. Struck with awe and fear, Jacob found himself at the "gate of heaven" beneath the "house of God". In a moment of divine grace, God reached out to Jacob with the same promise He had given to his grandfather Abraham and his father Isaac. God extended His unfathomable love to Jacob at a time when Jacob barely knew the Lord as his personal God. In the depth of Jacob's despair and fear, God reached out with a hope more wonderful than Jacob could have dreamed. His heavenly father promised security, protection, and significance to Jacob unilaterally, and Jacob made a vow in return. God honoured this vow, and twenty years later He reminded Jacob that He had indeed listened to Jacob's prayer (Genesis 31:13).

When We Reach Rock Bottom, God Takes Us Back to
the Top (Genesis 29-31)

Jacob's way of coping with his fears had so far brought him a lot of trouble. He needed to learn new ways of doing life, and the promise God had made to him was life-changing. He knew he could no longer continue to scheme and plot.

After fleeing his home, Jacob lived with his uncle Laban and worked for him. In Laban, Jacob saw a projection of himself, full of fear and insecurity. Laban also modelled Jacob's deception back to him, tricking his nephew into marrying his daughter Leah—whom Jacob did not desire—so the younger man would be forced to spend another seven years labouring in order to marry the daughter he really loved, Rachel. Laban further exploited Jacob by changing his working conditions and wages multiple times without consultation. But by learning to deal with Laban in a godly way, Jacob also learnt to change his own self-defeating ways of dealing with his own fears. Finally, Jacob was able to stand before Laban and declare:

> I have been with you for twenty years now. Your sheep and goats have not miscarried, nor have I eaten rams from your flocks. I did not bring you animals torn by wild beasts; I bore the loss myself. And you demanded payment from me for whatever was stolen by day or night. This was my situation: The heat consumed me in the daytime and the cold at night, and sleep fled from my eyes. It was like this for the twenty years I was in your household. I worked for you fourteen years for your two daughters and six years for your flocks, and you changed my wages ten times. If the God of my father, the God of Abraham and the Fear of Isaac, had not been with me, you would surely have sent me away empty-handed. But God has seen my hardship and the toil of my hands, and last night he rebuked you.
>
> — GENESIS 31:38-42

After twenty years, Jacob was no longer yielding to his fears in a counterproductive way. The Lord had prospered him and increased his significance and wealth because Jacob's maladaptive coping mechanisms for dealing with his fears were no longer hindering God's blessings upon him. It was at this point that God reminded Jacob of the vow he had made to Him at Bethel (Genesis 31:13). Now, Jacob was more than ready and equipped to wear the mantle of his grandfather Abraham and his father Isaac, which had been promised to him twenty years ago.

Healing from fears takes time. It had taken time for God to break down Jacob's negative ways of coping and to help him learn new behaviours. But there was one more fear that Jacob had to confront: his brother Esau and his threat of death. Jacob had found a firm faith in the God from whom he had obtained a sense of security and significance. But was that enough for him to confront Esau? Would Jacob continue to lean into God to deal with his fear?

With God's Help, We Can Face Our Fear (Genesis 32)

Jacob was understandably fearful about meeting his brother after all these years. He prepared lavish gifts for Esau, and he instructed his servants to clearly convey his subordination to his older brother. He also divided his household into two groups, each protecting its livestock, in case Esau attacked. He did everything humanly possible to prevent a show of conflict with Esau, and his behaviour displayed a genuine sense of remorse for his wrongdoings towards his brother. Jacob was in "great fear and distress" (verse 7), but he displayed responsible behaviour and humility in the hopes of preventing disaster and harm befalling his family.

Finally, Jacob prayed to God, acknowledging his own unworthiness, appealing to God's faithfulness, and asking for God's protection. But even this was not sufficient to quell his fear. He knew he had yet to confront his older brother Esau, and he knew that his mere presence would remind Esau of Jacob's deception in illegitimately obtaining the birthright and the blessings of their father, Isaac. Despite his wealth and the outward trappings of his significance, the impending encounter with Esau after more than twenty years reminds Jacob of his old inner insecurity and his fear of being insignificant.

In his moment of aloneness and time of vulnerability when every human protection was not available to him, Jacob's inner psyche and spirit were laid bare before God. His inner conflict left him no other alternative but to lean into God and grapple with these fears. In the stillness of the night and the depths of the darkness, Jacob physically wrestled with God. Every desire, every dream, and every fear were laid bare in the presence of the Lord Almighty. This was travailing at its fullness. There were no other beings there. No eyewitness to Jacob stepping into that tangible space with the Divine. Such transactions take place when God confronts us in a very personal way, and Jacob knew this was his only chance to wrestle it out. He would not let go until he received a blessing from God—a blessing that, when spoken, could be meant for no recipient but Jacob alone. It would not be a blessing that could be stolen or obtained by trickery. It must be a blessing that would give Jacob his legitimacy and finally deliver him from his fear.

The Lord did indeed bless Jacob and confirmed it by changing his name to Israel which means "he who struggles with God" (verse 28). By so doing, God gave Jacob a new identity and destiny, restoring his sense of legitimacy. Jacob knew then that he had seen God face to face (verse 30). This encounter with God was the climax of his dream at Bethel where he had found himself in the house of God (Genesis 28:17). He did not know God then, but now, on this occasion, he had encountered God and had wrestled with him man to man. Jacob's life was forever transformed. His walk with God would be as spiritually different as his physical walk was now different—for God also touched him with a limp so that he might know their encounter had been real. Now, instead of being a man full of fear, Jacob would live as a man who held the Fear of God. He had personally met with the God of his fathers, "the God of Abraham and the Fear of Isaac" (Genesis 31:42), and his life would never be the same.

Like Jacob, every fear we have needs to be resolved with our loving Father God. Our fears as humankind originated from the primal fears of death, rejection, abandonment, and loss of significance as a result of the Fall and the consequent estrangement from Father God. Like Jacob, we too need to lean into God hard, seeking His presence and His blessings. Our healing may be long and arduous, and we may need to confront the ways we deal with our fears as being unhelpful and even complicating our insecurities. We need to learn to yield to God's grace, so that we may find true freedom from our fear.

8

The Fatherhood of God in Mental Health and Healing

The Christian faith is unique compared to other spiritual faiths in its assertion of the fatherhood of God to believers. The fatherhood of God is implied in the narrative of Creation, recorded in Genesis in the Bible, where the origin of humankind can be traced back to God Himself. He created a human being out of the dust of the earth and breathed His own breath of life into the nostrils of the human (Genesis 1:26 and 2:7). Genesis 1 and 2 also describe a very close relationship between God and Adam and Eve, as He communicated and fellowshipped with them freely, and it was that relationship that was severed as a result of the Fall.

Beginning with the call of Abraham in Genesis 12, God worked out His plan to redeem a people group. From the individual Abraham came Abraham's son Isaac and his grandson Jacob, and then a people group called Israel. The relationship God intended for Himself and Israel is that of father and son. This is more specifically spelt out in Exodus 4:22-23, after God met Moses in the burning bush (Exodus 3). In that narrative—and subsequently written in other parts of the Bible—God described His relationship with Israel as one of a father and His firstborn son. The implication is that there will be many more children (Hebrews 2:10).

The quality of this father-and-son relationship is further elaborated in different passages of the Old Testament. To help the Israelites understand the nature of this relationship, God described it within the earthly experience of a father-and-son relationship, which is familiar to the Israelites. If you are a parent, you will resonate with this. A parent is loving, kind, protective, caring, forgiving, and sacrificial towards his children. The Bible describes the relationship of God and Israel in this fashion, and there are three verses in particular which resonate best with me:

"Is not Ephraim my dear son, the child in whom I delight? Though I often speak against him, I still remember him. Therefore my heart yearns for him; I have great compassion for him", declares the Lord.

— *JEREMIAH 31:20*

It was I who taught Ephraim to walk, taking them by the arms; but they did not realize it was I who healed them.

— *HOSEA 11:3*

The Lord your God is with you, the Mighty Warrior who saves. He will take great delight in you; in his love he will no longer rebuke you but will rejoice over you with singing.

— *ZEPHANIAH 3:17*

A good parent is one who is there for their children, whether those kids realise it or not. The parent is aware of each milestone of their offspring, no matter how small. The parent is strong and dependable, and every occasion with their kids is one of rejoicing, dancing, and celebration. This is how our heavenly father seeks to know us.

THE FATHERHOOD OF GOD AND JESUS

When Jesus was alive on earth, He was often referred to as the Son of God. In Matthew 2, Mary and Joseph escaped to Egypt to avoid an infant Jesus being killed by King Herod. They returned to their home with Jesus after King Herod's death. Matthew referenced the incident as the fulfillment of Hosea 11:1 which applies to the people of Israel as the son of God:

When they had gone, an angel of the Lord appeared to Joseph in a dream. "Get up," he said, "take the child and his mother and escape to Egypt. Stay there until I tell you, for Herod is going to search for the child to kill him." So he got up, took the child and his mother during the night, and left for Egypt, where he stayed until the death of Herod. And so was fulfilled what the Lord had said through the prophet: "Out of Egypt I called my son."

— MATTHEW 2:13-15

During the temptation of Jesus, even Satan referred to Jesus as the Son of God:

The tempter came to him and said, "If you are the Son of God, tell these stones to become bread."

— MATTHEW 4:3

Then the devil took him to the holy city and had him stand on the highest point of the temple. "If you are the Son of God," he said, "throw yourself down. For it is written: He will command his angels concerning you, and they will lift you up in their hands, so that you will not strike your foot against a stone."

— MATTHEW 4:5-6

On various occasions, Jesus also referred to Himself as the Son of God. In defence of His healing of the paralysed man by the pool at Bethesda, Jesus responded to the Jewish authorities as such:

Very truly I tell you, the Son can do nothing by himself; he can do only what he sees his Father doing, because whatever the Father does the Son also does. For the Father loves the Son and shows him all he does. Yes, and he will show him even greater works than these, so that you will be amazed. For just as the Father raises the dead and gives them life, even so the Son gives life to whom he is pleased to give it. Moreover, the Father judges no one, but has entrusted all judgement to the Son, that all may honour the Son just as they honour the Father. Whoever does not honour the Son does not honour the Father, who sent him.

— JOHN 5:19-23

THE FATHERHOOD OF GOD AND CHRISTIANS

Of the four authors of the Gospels, the Apostle John is the one who best developed the theme of believers being the sons of God. In John chapter one, he ties together the incarnation of the Word of God amongst humankind, the profession of faith in the Word of God, and the reality of becoming the sons of God:

In the beginning was the Word, and the Word was with God, and the Word was God. He was with God in the beginning. Through him all things were made; without him nothing was made that has been made. In him was life, and that life was the light of all mankind.

— JOHN 1:1-4

He came to that which was his own, but his own did not receive him. Yet to all who did receive him, to those who believed in his name, he gave the right to become children of God, children born not of natural descent, nor of human decision or a husband's will, but born of God.

— JOHN 1:11-13

John further connects the love of God and our calling as the sons of God, in 1 John 3:1:

See what great love the Father has lavished on us, that we should be called children of God!

He also wrote in 1 John 4:10:

This is love: not that we loved God, but that he loved us and sent his Son as an atoning sacrifice for our sins.

Our sonship is made possible by the redemptive work of Jesus Christ on the cross of Calvary. He has not only paid the price for our sins but has enabled us to be adopted into the family of God. When Mary Magdalene met Jesus on the first resurrection Sunday, John recorded the following:

Jesus said to her, "Mary." She turned toward him and cried out in Aramaic, "Rabboni!" (which means "Teacher"). Jesus said, "Do not hold on to me, for I have not yet ascended to the Father. Go instead to my brothers and tell them, 'I am ascending to my Father and your Father, to my God and your God."

— JOHN 20:16-17

Later, the Apostle Paul elaborated on the teaching of our adoption in his writings in Romans:

Therefore, brothers and sisters, we have an obligation—but it is not to the flesh, to live according to it. For if you live according to the flesh, you will die; but if by the Spirit you put to death the misdeeds of the body, you will live. For those who are led by the Spirit of God are the children of God. The Spirit you received does not make you slaves, so that you live in fear again; rather, the Spirit you received brought about your adoption to sonship. And by him we cry, "Abba, Father."

— ROMANS 8:12-15

He then reinforces the idea of the adoption of our sonship in Galatians 4:1-7:

What I am saying is that as long as an heir is underage, he is no different from a slave, although he owns the whole estate. The heir is subject to guardians and trustees until the time set by his father. So also, when we were underage, we were in slavery under the elemental spiritual forces of the world. But when the set time had fully come, God sent his Son, born of a woman, born under the law, to redeem those under the law, that we might receive adoption to sonship. Because you are his sons, God sent the Spirit of his Son into our hearts, the Spirit who calls out, 'Abba, Father.' So you are no longer a slave, but God's child; and since you are his child, God has made you also an heir.

Salvation therefore is not just to be set free from sin and its curses but to be adopted into the family of God. We are not merely sinners saved by grace—though that is truth. But the grace of God is more than that. His purpose is better and so much more. His intention is for us—mere mortals that we are—to be adopted by Him so that we can be called the sons of God, heirs and joint heirs with Christ. As it is declared in the Scriptures:

Now if we are children, then we are heirs—heirs of God and co-heirs with Christ, if indeed we share in his sufferings in order that we may also share in his glory.

— ROMANS 8:17

I am blown away whenever I read this verse. Imagine this for a moment with me: Everything that Jesus is, I am; everything that Jesus has, I have. Let us ponder this truth.

THE FATHERHOOD OF GOD AND HEALING

One of the important revelations in the Scriptures is the identity of God as the Healer. God first revealed His identity as the Healer in Exodus 15:26:

If you listen carefully to the Lord your God and do what is right in his eyes, if you pay attention to his commands and keep all his decrees, I will not bring on you any of the diseases I brought on the Egyptians, for I am the Lord, who heals you.

The context of this passage is the children of Israel wandering in the Desert of Shur for three days without water. Finally, they found a stream, but the water was too bitter to drink. As usual, they grumbled and complained to Moses. The Lord then instructed Moses to throw a piece of wood into the stream, and after that the water was fit to drink.

On this occasion, the Lord revealed Himself as Jehovah Rapha—Jehovah the Healer. The Hebraic meaning of the word "rapha" is to restore or to heal. Throughout the Old Testament, there are many references to the Lord being the Healer. He is the Healer of our diseases, the Restorer of our health, and the Repairer of our emotional wounds:

Praise the Lord, my soul, and forget not all his benefits—who forgives all your sins and heals all your diseases.

— PSALM 103:2-3

"But I will restore you to health and heal your wounds," declares the Lord, "because you are called an outcast, Zion for whom no one cares."

— JEREMIAH 30:17

He heals the broken hearted and binds up their wounds.

— PSALM 147:3

Nevertheless, I will bring health and healing to it; I will heal my people and will let them enjoy abundant peace and security.

— JEREMIAH 33:6

The Lord is close to the broken hearted and saves those who are crushed in spirit.

— PSALM 34:18

God's healing for His children is not confined to the spiritual—it extends to the physical, emotional, and mental as well. Isaiah, anticipating the redemptive work of the Messiah, wrote in the often-quoted verses of Isaiah 53:4-5:

Surely he took up our pain and bore our suffering, yet we considered him punished by God, stricken by Him, and afflicted. But he was pierced for our transgressions, he was crushed for our iniquities, the punishment that brought us peace was on Him, and by his wounds we are healed.

Isaiah also foreshadowed the healing work of the Messiah in Isaiah 61:1:

The Spirit of the Sovereign Lord is on me, because the Lord has anointed me to proclaim good news to the poor. He has sent me to

*bind up the broken hearted, to proclaim freedom for the captives and
release from darkness for the prisoners.*

The ministry of the Messiah is not only one of redemption for people
from their sins, but also one of emotional healing from mental health
problems. Matthew affirmed Jesus' ministry as the Messiah in Matthew 8:16
and 17, where he wrote that Jesus had driven out evil spirits and "healed
all the sick" as a fulfilment of Isaiah 61:1. Matthew also added, "He took up
our infirmities and bore our diseases" (verse 17).

We know from the Scriptures that Jesus' ministry is as much the healing
of the emotionally sick or mentally oppressed as it is the healing of the
physically inflicted. Jesus' famous teaching on the Beatitudes is primarily a
pathway to better mental health (Matthew 5:3-10). He also invites us to be
in partnership with Him so that we can relieve ourselves of our emotional
burdens:

*Come to me, all you who are weary and burdened, and I will give you
rest. Take my yoke upon you and learn from me, for I am gentle and
humble in heart, and you will find rest for your souls. For my yoke is
easy and my burden is light.*

— *MATTHEW 11:28-30*

In Luke 8:26-39 and the parallel passage in Mark 5:1-20, Jesus healed
the demon-possessed man at Gerasene by driving out the evil spirits from
his body. As a result, the man's mind was also restored. The villagers found
him dressed and "in his right mind" (Luke 8:35). In this case, the demon
possession had affected the person's mind as well as his body. Ridding him
of the evil spirits helped restore him to better physical and mental health.

In the often-quoted passage of John 21:15-19, Jesus reaffirmed Peter after
his denial of Jesus (Matthew 26:31-35). Three times, Jesus asked Peter if he
loved Him. The three queries correspond to Peter's denial of Jesus, which
he did three times. There are many ways to interpret this passage, but for
me, this is a very beautiful passage of inner healing offered by Jesus to Peter.

We know from the Scriptures that Peter was a person who wore his heart on his sleeve. He made no pretence about his feelings, and he was indeed overcome with remorse regarding his denial of Jesus. After he had denied Jesus three times and the rooster crowed, Peter "went out and wept bitterly" (Luke 22:54-62). It is highly probable that Peter had unresolved guilt over his denial of Jesus, but he likely also had a moment of epiphany about his own frailty and weakness, and the shallowness of his love for Jesus. After all, he had shown he would not die for his Master as he had previously claimed he would.

In the first two instances of Jesus asking Peter if he loved Him, Jesus was referring to "agape" love—love of the highest sacrificial order. Peter could only reply twice that he loved Jesus with a brotherly type of love, which is considered a lower order of love. On the third occasion, Jesus changed His question to ask if Peter loved Him with that brotherly love. Peter "was grieved". He responded, "Lord, you know everything; you know that I love you" (John 21:17).

In this beautiful exchange, Jesus revealed Peter's true self—a part of himself that he did not know before. Jesus needed Peter to know more about himself before he could be commissioned to the next calling in his life. Yet despite this confronting inner look, Jesus interacted with Peter in such a gentle way that Peter was released from his guilt. In its place, he found forgiveness, acceptance, and belonging.

THE MINISTRY OF JESUS

The Bible says that God spoke through His prophets in diverse times in the past. But God's final spokesperson is none other than His Son, Jesus Christ (Hebrews 1:1-4). Jesus said that He is "the Way, the Truth and the Life," and it is through Him that we come to the Father (John 14:6). When we know Jesus, we also know the Father (John 14:9), with Jesus claiming that He and the Father are one (John 10:30). Essentially, Jesus revealed His unity and oneness with the Father in the Godhead. The Son and the Father enjoy such intimacy that they are one being, and their relationship is characterised by synchrony, unity, and deep intimacy. Humanly speaking, the Son knows the very heartbeat of the Father.

Through Jesus and His redemptive death on the cross of Calvary, Christ made it possible for each of us to enjoy the same intimacy with the Father. We can come close to the father-heart of God, as Jesus does. Jesus described this mystical but real experience in His prayer in John chapter 17:

> *My prayer is not for them alone. I pray also for those who will believe in me through their message, that all of them may be one, Father, just as you are in me, and I am in you. May they also be in us so that the world may believe that you have sent me. I have given them the glory that you gave me, that they may be one as we are one—I in them and you in me—so that they may be brought to complete unity. Then the world will know that you sent me and have loved them even as you have loved me.*
>
> — *JOHN 17:20-23*

This divine intimacy, which originates from the father-heart of God, is extended to all people. Often, people with mental health problems suffer from a sense of rejection, non-belonging, a lack of intimacy, and alienation. Yet humans are made to connect (Genesis 2:18). We cannot exist by ourselves. We need significant others to establish a sense of our selfhood and our meaning in life. Our selfhood is complete when it is rightly complemented by a meaningful connectedness with others.

People who have good connections generally enjoy better mental health than those who are isolated and alienated. Access to the father-heart of God through intimacy can help heal one's mental health problems because it increases a sense of acceptance and belonging. God has made this possible by first reconciling us to Himself through Jesus Christ (2 Corinthians 5:18), and then making us feel accepted and that we belong through His adoption of us into sonship (Ephesians 1:5).

Through acceptance and belonging, we also have peace with God (Romans 5:1) and the peace of God (John 14:27). Mental health problems often rob us of a sense of peace. The conflict of the soul and the disquiet of the spirit accompany sufferers of depression, anxiety, and fear. This is often manifested in the disturbance of one's bodily functions, creating poor sleep, motor activities and thought processes. Psychotropic medications often fail to calm the person, only numbing them instead. This means the person feels anaesthetised against their psychic pain, but it also dulls their positive emotions. Most of my patients find this experience so intolerable that they take themselves off their medications. Peace that is accessed through the father-heart of God is different. It is refreshing, energising, and motivating (Psalm 23).

People with mental health problems often feel hopeless. It is a core feature of depressed patients, yet the Scriptures promise us that hope is accessible through the father-heart of God:

> *And hope does not put us to shame, because God's love has been poured out into our hearts through the Holy Spirit, who has been given to us.*
> — ROMANS 5:5

The hope that we have in Father God is a result of our knowledge of His unconditional love for us. The more we are convinced of His love for us, the firmer our hope is placed in Him. This hope is not built on our own efforts and plans but is firmly rooted in His faithfulness. Thus, our spirit is able to declare with genuine hope:

> *Because of the Lord's great love we are not consumed, for his compassions never fail. They are new every morning; great is your faithfulness. I say to myself, "The Lord is my portion therefore I will wait for him." The Lord is good to those whose hope is in him, to the one who seeks him, it is good to wait quietly for the salvation of the Lord.*
> — LAMENTATIONS 3:22-26

This is also the sort of hope which helps us to transcend difficult and challenging circumstances.

But those who hope in the Lord will renew their strength. They will soar on wings like eagles; they will run and not grow weary, they will walk and not be faint.

— ISAIAH 40:31

Ultimately, our mental health and deliverance from psychiatric problems—whether anxiety, fear, or depression—culminates in a personal knowledge of God and His loving heart for us.

~

Congratulations—you have made it through Part 1 of this book! I hope you have enjoyed our journey together exploring mental health, anxiety problems and fear, the biopsychosocial treatment and its limitations, and the necessity of considering and treating anxiety problems and fear from a Christian spiritual perspective. I hope you have managed to learn a little more about me, both personally and professionally, through my own testimonies and the case studies I've shared with you.

If you are like me, you may be saying to yourself, "So what? What do I actually do with the knowledge gained from Part 1?" When I am told about a problem, I also like to be told how to fix it. I am into self-help. I feel empowered after working through a manual to successfully fix a problem, and as a therapist, I believe in empowering other people as well. In fact, when I first began writing this book, it started as an abridged version of Part 2—basically like a little manual. So now we have arrived at what I first intended: a self-help manual to deal with anxiety and fear from a Christian spiritual perspective.

Like a lot of people, when I have an IKEA manual in my hands, I tend to skip over things or make certain assumptions about how to put the bits and pieces together. Inevitably I get frustrated and confused, only to find I must dismantle everything and begin anew. With that in mind, I advise you to read the following chapters in a consecutive manner, as the skills you will learn are meant to build upon one another. I would also suggest that you try out the various exercises as you go along. Whether or not you struggle with anxiety or fear, the exercises will enrich your mental health and spiritual life. You can even share the practices you learn with your friends, colleagues, and loved ones.

PART TWO

Skills for Optimising Mental Health

9

Be Aware

Most people find it difficult to tolerate anxious feelings. This is because anxiety is associated with a state of unease or apprehension characterised by a heightened sense of worry, nervousness, or fear. It often involves a sense of impending danger or threat, even when there may not be any immediate or concrete reason for such feelings. Instinctively—and especially if they have not experienced anxious feelings before—most people react to anxious feelings as a noxious emotion and seek to get rid of it as quickly as possible.

Fear is usually associated with an object or situation that we can name, and thus can reasonably retreat from or deal with on the spot. So, when fear comes out of the blue and we cannot link it to a specific threat or our current situation, it is called a panic or anxiety attack. But humans seek to understand and interpret their experiences, which is why the great majority of people who experience a panic attack for the first time will often think they are having a heart attack. It is not uncommon for many to present to the nearest hospital or their family doctor, as the inexplicable aspect of the physical sensations of fear can lead them to expect the worst. Many who have experienced acute anxiety in the form of a panic attack experience fear to the point where they become physically unwell whenever anxiety rears its head. This may escalate until they experience wave upon wave of overwhelming anxiety. Had they learned effective calming techniques, the anxiety may have settled after a short time.

Those who suffer from a chronic anxiety disorder will tell you they feel constantly on edge, stressed and tense, while others have a sense of perpetual restlessness. Their brains are constantly filled with worries and concerns, and these worries seem to have a life of their own, acting as though on autopilot mode irrespective of whether or not the person intended to worry in the first place. Still others complain that their brains are constantly foggy as though they are thinking through a thick cloud.

The first step in the management of anxiety, acute or chronic, is to teach the person to respond rather than react to the anxiety. This is often quite an effort. The reason is that, by the time the person decides to seek help, they have already conditioned themselves to treat the anxious feeling as an undesirable emotion. They therefore have to unlearn the behaviours which perpetuate the anxiety in the first place. To do this, the person must take a number of steps backwards, starting with learning to be aware of their anxious feeling without reacting to them. This can be a difficult skill to master, as we live in an "instant" world. We do business at the speed of light. We have not learnt how to pause, and we expect our problems to be solved yesterday.

But before you can learn to be this type of self-aware, you first need to consider some new knowledge which you may or may not have come across before.

1. Physical Sensations Precede Emotions

As living creatures, we are constantly responding and reacting to our external world and our internal being, through our five senses: smell, touch, sight, taste, and hearing. Upon the amalgamation of these physical and psychological sensations, we can then label our state of being with "feeling" words which we call emotions. For example, when faced with a wild animal, our heart rate goes up, we perspire profusely, we experience extreme muscle tension, and we breathe faster and heavier while our mind thinks up a thousand ways to flee. We label the aggregation of these sensations as "fear". Now let us imagine going on a first date with a person we have secretly adored for some time. With that much-desired person now in close proximity, our heart rate goes up, we perspire, and our breathing becomes faster. Our pupils dilate, and in our mind we imagine a thousand ways to impress this person. We do not wish to flee, but we long to linger and savour every moment of this intoxicating experience, even as it leaves us "weak at the knees". This time, we label the aggregate of these physical sensations as "romance".

In both situations described above, the physiological responses giving rise to the physical reactions are the same. Yet, due to the different scenarios of these two experiences, we label the subsequent emotions very differently—one is fear while the other is romance. The context makes all the difference.

2. Emotions Are Neither Good nor Bad

Flowing on from this knowledge, we can also assert that emotions are neither good nor bad in themselves. They are just the cumulated result of our bodily sensations as we interact with our environment. Our ability to manage emotions is more important than the simple judgement of whether they are "good or bad". In fact, the judgement of emotions often hinders their management and makes them more unpleasant. If emotions are only signals regarding a situation, then anxiety is merely a signal that we are stepping into a situation of uncertainty. An extreme example of such a situation is when our physical or psychological integrity is actively threatened. In the case of feeling acutely anxious when walking down a dark alleyway, we could regard that emotion as helpful, seeing as it serves to make us more alert. That alertness, along with a heightened sense of vigilance, is welcome, as we are unsure of our physical surroundings and whether or not our safety might be compromised. However, the same physical sensations landing in the form of a panic attack often throw us off guard, because there is no sign of imminent danger. The emotional experience of extreme fear—despite our physical or psychological self not being under threat—can leave us confused and disoriented. Our bodily sensations tell us that we need to get away from an imminent threat, but we do not know what that threat is.

I have been treating patients with panic disorder for many years. Most if not all of my patients tell me that when they experience their first panic attack, they have a strong urge to run away or escape from something which they cannot pinpoint. Most end up "running away" from the situation itself, even though they have experienced—or even enjoyed—the same situation many times before. In this case, the cognitive appraisal of the situation does not match the severity of the physical sensations. The experience of fear during this "attack" can be so severe, that the majority of my patients retain a body memory of the physical sensations associated with that scenario. The proposal of future exposure to the same place or situation therefore tends to elicit further feelings of fear, though to a milder degree, and avoidance becomes the usual next step for the person. But if the avoidance continues and is left untreated, the person could develop a secondary psychiatric disorder such as agoraphobia, social anxiety disorder, or specific phobia.

3. Our Response to an Anxious Feeling is More Important than the Anxious Feeling Itself

An anxious feeling is simply a response to situations or events in which the outcome is uncertain—real or perceived. For example, a student might feel rather anxious about an upcoming examination, uncertain if he has studied enough to pass. His friend, on the other hand, may be feeling calm and quite confident, believing he will pass with flying colours as he knows he has spent a great deal of time preparing for this examination. In the case of the former, the anxious student may be able to change his anxious feelings into confidence if he decides to buckle down and put in some extra hard work. But should he decide that it is already *fait accompli* and that no amount of effort will make any difference, then he might even feel quite depressed about the examination.

But what about anxiety that is more severe than the subtle feelings of concern that most of us experience as a normal part of daily life? Let's take the example of a panic attack. The reaction to a panic attack occurring in one's own body and mind is normally catastrophic—nothing can prepare a person for what it is like to feel such a deep level of strident, hopeless fear. Unfortunately, as long as the person continues to react so intensely, no matter how many times they have experienced such attacks before, the panic disorder will persist. The reason for this is the body's natural response to a "catastrophe", which is to produce huge bursts of adrenaline and noradrenaline to "fight" whatever is causing the panic attack. The person becomes hyper-aroused and even more agitated, but the cause of the panic is not resolved. This keeps the levels of adrenaline consistently high in preparation for the next "attack", which results in the person experiencing rolling anxiety. It's a vicious cycle. Not only that but, in the longer term, the person will also likely develop secondary disorders such as depression or agoraphobia (anxiety disorder).

Throughout my years as a psychiatrist, I have treated many patients with panic disorder. They tell me that the feeling of impending doom and catastrophe is so real that it is hard not to react with anything other than terror. It is as though there is a cognitive dissonance between what they are feeling and what is actually happening. The person feels utterly terrified even though there is no real disaster or impending catastrophe, which leaves them confused as to how to act. This is why a person will often end up "running away" from the situation or immediate environment. The very real emotion of terror and impending doom, and the confusion of logically knowing nothing is visibly wrong, pushes them to withdraw from the situation altogether. "The anxiety will go away," they hypothesise, "when I can get away from this situation." The reality is that most of us do not instinctively know how to manage our way through a catastrophically anxious situation without being taught how to do it.

4. The Best Way to Stay Calm When You are Feeling Anxious is *not* to Stay in the Anxious Emotion

Suppose I asked you to change the state of your present emotion from one to another at random. How would you do it? Suppose you were feeling sad and I asked you to feel happy. How do you change from feeling anxious to feeling calm and peaceful? It is incredibly hard to force yourself to feel one way, when every sensation feeding into your body is telling you to feel another way entirely—especially if the feeling is very negative, whether it is anxiety, nervousness, fear, sadness, or anger.

In my practice as a child and adolescent psychiatrist, I teach young people to count to 10 and to walk away from a situation which is associated with an immensely negative emotion. I ask them to call a "Time Out", and to remove themselves from the situation—physically if possible, and if not, then psychologically in their mind. The young person is further taught to recognise the situation which triggers the negative emotion, to be aware of and name the emotion, and then to pre-empt a "Time Out" whenever that emotion seeks to rear its head.

With the above understanding and explanation, let's now focus on how to manage our fear and anxiety. There are six key steps in this exercise. The first step is *Be Aware*. It is further broken down into these sub-steps:

1. Recognising the physical sensations which herald the emotions of fear and anxiety.
2. Correctly labelling the emotions of fear and anxiety without judgement.
3. Calling a "Time Out".

Let's deal with acute anxiety or fear first.

ACUTE ANXIETY

When managing acute anxiety, we need to understand the importance of:

1. Accurately Recognising the Bodily Sensations of Acute Anxiety

The bodily sensations of acute anxiety or fear are:

- Increased heart rate, which you may experience as a heavy thumping in your chest—it can be quite uncomfortable.
- Fast breathing, as though you have just engaged in arduous exercise. You may find you have difficulty catching your breath.

- Profuse sweating, as though you have just been labouring physically in the hot sun.

- Increased muscle tension with a feeling as though your muscles are coiled and cannot relax. You may feel like you need to be physically active to discharge the muscle tension from your body.

- Chest tightness, as though someone has put a heavy weight on top of it. When a person experiences their first acute anxiety attack or panic attack, the chest tightness is so painful that they often mistake the sensation for a heart attack. This person will often present to the family physician or the accident and emergency department of a hospital to have their heart checked.

- A lump in the throat, making it feel as though you cannot breathe. This feeling is a result of muscle contractions around the throat. The perceived inability to breathe feels very frightening, and the person may think he or she is about to die from asphyxiation. I often have to reassure my patients that they will not die from asphyxiation, no matter how severe the tight feeling in their throat is, unless someone is literally strangling them.

- Dizziness, as though you are about to pass out.

- Pins and needles sensations in the extremities of the hands or around the mouth. Sometimes, the person experiences a tingling sensation in all their extremities.

- A feeling of unshakeable doom and gloom, as though a disaster is about to hit. This heavy feeling is often out of context with the actual situation the person is in.

- Racing thoughts which are out of your control, making it hard to focus and concentrate on a single thought.

The above symptoms are all a result of having too much adrenaline and noradrenaline in the body, coupled with an increased breathing rate which changes the chemical property of the blood circulation. At the moment of acute anxiety or fear, it is important for the person not to overreact to the bodily sensations. If you experience these symptoms, it is important to recognise them as signals that you are experiencing an acute anxiety attack or extreme fear. You may want to pause and get yourself in a comfortable position or situation, but there is no need to panic or run away from the situation you are in unless the scene is so overwhelming that it exacerbates the symptoms. If the situation permits a pause, you may choose to stop whatever you are doing and find a quiet place to sit down in preparation for the next steps.

2. Correctly Labelling the Emotions of Fear and Anxiety Without Judgement

The next step in the management of acute anxiety or fear is to label the aggregate of the physical sensations with "feelings" words. Do not attempt to explain *how* the feeling has been triggered, or whether you should feel one way or another. Simple statements which are precise and concise— such as those below—should suffice. It is also helpful to speak aloud in a soft voice so that you can hear your own statements. For example, try saying aloud:

"I am feeling anxious."
"This is an anxious feeling."
"I am having an anxiety attack."
"I am feeling panicky."

3. Calling a Time Out

There are two steps to calling a "Time Out". Firstly, you must not engage with the anxiety—refrain from any debate or judgement about what you are feeling. Secondly, direct your attention inward towards imagery which encourages you to wait for the acute anxiety to abate. I call this approach *Wait, Watch and Wonder.*

Step One: Refraining from Judgement and Debate

This is the part that is initially difficult to achieve because all your thoughts are actively insisting that all is not well. You are likely to have sudden thoughts like, "I am going to die", "Something terrible is happening here", and "I am going to have a heart attack" etc. But the more you dwell on these thoughts, the more your body remains in fight-flight mode, leading to more outpouring of stress hormones such as adrenaline and noradrenaline which perpetuated the initial acute anxiety attack.

In my practice as a child, adolescent and family psychiatrist, I have treated numerous patients who suffered from panic disorders, and who were unfortunately taught to engage with their anxious thoughts by debating their rationality. The idea with this approach is that anxious thoughts begat anxious feelings—replacing the anxious thoughts with non-anxious ones should therefore extinguish the anxious feeling. However, my patients tell me that they don't *feel* any different even though they can logically judge, debate, and replace their anxious thoughts. Worse still, some of them actually feel more agitated by engaging with their thoughts. Some even say they feel angry with themselves that nothing has changed despite their strenuous efforts to correct their unhelpful thoughts.

My conclusion is that a state of calm cannot be achieved when one has to busily engage with already racing thoughts. Indeed, many of my patients report that they find it difficult to control their thought processes at all during such an episode. Disengagement, rather than engagement, is what allows the thoughts to slow down and—after a while—to settle, which leads me to step two of the "Time Out" approach.

Step Two: Wait, Watch and Wonder

Mental imagery which includes movement but is associated with a different emotional outcome helps to alleviate anxiety. Allow me to elaborate.

An example of simple mental imagery is to visualise oneself out on the ocean, riding the surf. You're floating on a board in the rolling blue, watching and waiting as the current pulls you back towards the shore. The visual imagery of a wave or surf matches the actual physical experience of many who experience acute anxiety attacks. They often describe themselves as being hit by "a wave" of anxiety. In the case of this mental imagery, one can maintain a neutral stance of curiosity, waiting and wondering when the surf will end. Watching helps one to maintain an observer stance, while wondering deflects one from the foregone conclusion of disaster. Fight-flight hormones are like a surge coming in. We need to maintain a sense of curiosity—this is going to disappear and dissipate—rather than fighting it. Otherwise, our body will produce more fight-flight hormones, resulting in another wave of anxiety which leads to "rolling anxiety". This is when we get anxious about the anxiety, and incidentally accentuate the fight-flight hormones with successive waves of anxiety. What started as one wave can all too soon become overwhelming, creating a self-fulfilling prophecy that the situation really is out of control and leading us towards extreme fear.

The biblical narrative of Jesus calming the storm in Mark 4:35-39 provides a very powerful visual imagery of *Wait, Watch and Wonder*:

> *That day when evening came, he said to his disciples, "Let us go over to the other side." Leaving the crowd behind, they took him along, just as he was, in the boat. There were also other boats with him. A furious squall came up, and the waves broke over the boat, so that it was nearly swamped. Jesus was in the stern, sleeping on a cushion. The disciples woke him and said to him, "Teacher, don't you care if we drown?"*
> *He got up, rebuked the wind, and said to the waves, "Quiet! Be still!" Then the wind died down and it was completely calm.*

In this well-known passage of waves, turmoil, fear and anxiety, having Jesus onboard results in a different-than-expected outcome. Many of my Christian patients have found this passage helpful in the *Wait, Watch and Wonder* exercise. It helps the individual to detract from the anticipated negative outcomes of an acute anxiety attack. Some read the passage using a Bible App on their phone, immersing themselves in the narrative. Others who are better at visualisation simply imagine themselves as one of the disciples on the boat, being tossed by the waves but looking to Jesus with a curious anticipation that He will calm the waves. Still others repeat the words of Jesus: "Peace, be still."

~

Before I move on to talk about chronic anxiety, here is a brief review of what we have learnt about acute anxiety. To recap, the steps to *Be Aware* when feeling acutely fearful or anxious are:

1. Recognise the bodily sensations of acute anxiety.
2. Correctly label it as an emotion by saying, "I am feeling anxious."
3. Accept the anxious feeling without debate or judgement.
4. Elicit mental or visual imagery of riding a gentle surf or of Jesus calming the storm.
5. Allow yourself to Wait, Watch and Wonder as you focus on the mental imagery.

CHRONIC ANXIETY

When an acute anxiety disorder is not adequately treated, it becomes chronic. Unlike acute anxiety, chronic anxiety is not as strong. The person is not usually hit with a wave of panic, but rather experiences a constant sense of disquiet and angst. Unable to achieve a sense of inner calm and peace, they often feel a sense of inner restlessness. A sufferer of chronic anxiety may find it hard to fully enjoy life. Some may even complain of worrying thoughts over things that are rather trivial and insignificant. Many of these patients are rightly diagnosed with generalised anxiety disorder. They wake up worrying about the day before it has begun. For these people, the following two 'Be Aware' exercises, in addition to 'Watch, Wait and Wonder' will be beneficial.

Five Senses Five Minutes—A "Be Aware" Exercise

It is good and even vital to continue with the *Be Aware* exercise after the crisis is over. The more we can be aware of negative and distressing emotions without reacting to them, the better our mental health becomes. Following on from this, the *Five Senses Five Minutes* exercise helps to sharpen our awareness of our bodily sensations. This exercise is not one of emptying our minds. On the contrary, it is an exercise of intentional focus.

The steps for *Five Senses Five Minutes* are as below:

1. Pick an emotionally neutral place that is not overly stimulating. It may be the garden at the back of your house, a quiet park, or a nearby beach.
2. Take a deep breath in and out, and close your eyes (unless you are doing a visual sensory exercise).
3. Scan your own body from the top of your head to the tips of your toes, slowly and progressively picking up on any sensation that your sight, hearing, touch, smell, and taste bring to your attention.
4. Focus on that sensation without interpretation and judgement.
5. Label the sensation, e.g. "That is a green leaf" (sight), "I can feel the warmth of the sunlight on my skin" (touch), and "That's a bird singing" (hearing).
6. Focus on each sensory stimulus in a neutral way, noticing its effect on your faculty without judgement.
7. Slowly shift your awareness to another stimulus when you feel ready to move on from the first stimulus.

Becoming intentionally aware of our bodily sensations is the first step towards managing our anxiety and emotional regulation. I suggest doing this exercise for about five minutes each day. You could incorporate it into your daily devotion time or Bible reading, practice it on your way to and from work, or add it to your list of daily habits such as brushing your teeth, having a shower, and making a cup of tea.

Five Attributes Five Minutes—A "Be Aware" Exercise

Using the *Five Senses Five Minutes* exercise above, I have further taught my Christian patients to extend the exercise to intentionally focus on five attributes of God—His love, faithfulness, mercy, goodness, and grace. I call this the *Five Attributes Five Minutes* exercise. Many of my Christian patients become less anxious as they learn to focus on and see the love, mercy, faithfulness, goodness, and grace of God unfolding in their daily lives. To practice the *Five Attributes Five Minutes* exercise, follow the steps below:

1. Pick an emotionally neutral place that is not overly stimulating. It may be the garden at the back of your house, a quiet park, or a nearby beach.
2. Take a deep breath in and out, and close your eyes (unless you are doing a visual sensory exercise).
3. Scan your own body from the top of your head to the tips of your toes, slowly and progressively picking up on any sensation that your sight, hearing, touch, smell, and taste bring to your attention.
4. Focus on that sensation without interpretation and judgement.
5. Label the sensation, e.g. "That is a green leaf" (sight), "I can feel the warmth of the sunlight on my skin" (touch), and "That's a bird singing" (hearing).
6. Focus on each sensory stimulus in a neutral way, noticing its effect on your faculty without judgement.
7. Slowly shift your awareness to consider an attribute of God. Which attribute does the sensory stimulus remind you of? For example, the warmth of the sunlight on your skin might remind you of His love. The sight of beautiful flowers or majestic trees might remind you of His goodness and care.
8. Once you have decided on an attribute of God, allow yourself to be totally immersed in it, whether it is love, faithfulness, goodness, mercy, or grace.
9. Say a short prayer to finish the exercise: For example, "Father,

thank You for Your love for me. Help me to experience Your love today as I go about my day. In Your Son's name I pray. Amen."

10. Journal your experiences as you practice these exercises. This will help you to see how you are progressing in managing your anxiety and fear.

The *Wait, Watch and Wonder, Five Minutes Five Senses,* and *Five Attributes Five Minutes* exercises can all be used to reduce our daily stresses. In fact, doing these exercises routinely could help prevent a fear or anxiety problem from developing. As I frequently share with my patients, we live in a highly stressful and isolating world, and we need to know how to de-stress in a healthy way. Learning to be aware is the first step towards better mental health.

10

Anchoring

The main theme of anxiety and fear is one of uncertainty. In the case of separation anxiety, we are uncertain about how we'll cope when separated from our source of security, while with social anxiety, the uncertainty relates to our perceived inability to display proper social behaviours that are acceptable to others. In some anxiety disorders, the uncertainty relates to the fear that our physical integrity might be compromised or something harmful might happen. One example which is well known to many of us is the compulsive hand washing behaviour that comes with a obsessive compulsive disorder related to the fear of germs. In this case, we are not certain that our hands are clean enough, fearing they may still be contaminated with germs despite excessive and careful handwashing, which could result in us falling sick. In the more severe anxiety disorder of post-traumatic stress disorder, whenever our traumatic memory is triggered, we genuinely fear that we are about to be harmed and our physical integrity compromised.

Whilst the physiological symptoms of fear and anxiety are expressed in our bodies through the fight-flight response, the notion of uncertainty is expressed as worrying thoughts. In the case of a panic attack, these thoughts quickly become overwhelming and frightening. Some examples are:

"I am going to die!"
"Something bad is about to happen to me."

"I have to escape from here right now."
"Nobody can help me."

In the case of an obsessive compulsive disorder, the most common compulsive behaviours are repetitive cleaning, checking, or counting to a special number. Meanwhile, the worrying thoughts behind all this could be:

"If I don't clean myself thoroughly, I will get very sick from
the germs."
"If I don't check all the electrical power points, the house will
burn down."
"If I don't count to ten when I leave this room, something bad
will happen to my loved ones."

Having worrying thoughts is a universal experience which I dare say none of us have escaped at some stage or other. For example, many of us have worried about a plane crash. But despite this concern, we can reason with ourselves that it rarely happens, brush the worrying thought aside and travel by air regardless. It becomes a fear, however, when we are utterly convinced it will happen to us, and we stop flying as a precaution. Thus, our worrying thoughts become a mental health problem when they take over our ability to lead an optimal life. In other cases, our worrying thoughts are totally unrelated to the actions we may take to prevent a negative outcome. It immediately becomes obvious this is a mental health problem. Obsessive compulsive disorders fall into this category, for example in counting to a special number to prevent a disaster—we cannot logically fathom or explain how the special number has anything to do with the disaster, yet we are convinced it must be so.

Clearly, these worrying thoughts do not represent the actual reality of the situation but are instead the result of having too much adrenaline on board, triggering the fight-flight response. Unfortunately, to the person being flooded with adrenaline, these disasters feel very real. Most of us accept that life is full of uncertainties and not everything is under our control, but those of us who suffer from anxiety disorders and fear give in to that minuscule possibility that the bad consequences we worry about *will* happen. We feel trapped, anticipating imminent danger and awful catastrophe, and we cope by giving in to our fear—but fear breeds fear. And all too soon it can dominate and control our lives. Then we become enslaved to fear and fear becomes our master. This is why we all need to learn to manage our worrying thoughts, no matter how small or insignificant they may seem. Let us begin by learning a few important things about thoughts.

1. Thoughts are Thoughts, Thoughts are Not Reality

The first thing we need to learn about thoughts is this: Thoughts are not reality. Thought itself is a product of the neuronal activities of our brain. It is something metaphysical. Thoughts live inside our minds, and we are the master. They can, however, influence the ways we interpret our experiences, perceive reality, and formulate a response to those experiences. For example, most of us will react with a startled response on hearing "gunshots", thinking for a moment that danger is imminent. But the perception of danger is inside our mind, and we quickly locate the external reality that the "gunshot" noises were actually firecrackers being set off by our neighbours.

Let's consider a common anxiety disorder from which many of us suffer, called social anxiety disorder. The main characteristics of social anxiety disorder are:

- The person experiences overwhelming anxiety or fear in social situations, particularly those involving interaction with others or the potential for scrutiny or judgement.
- The person experiences a persistent fear of being embarrassed, humiliated, or negatively evaluated by others.
- The person often goes to great lengths to avoid situations that trigger their anxiety.

The main reason behind social anxiety is the fear of being criticised, judged, or humiliated by others; the result is social avoidance. For those of us who suffer from social anxiety, the emotional pain of deciding to attend a social function is excruciating. We preoccupy ourselves with what we should wear, how and when we should talk, and the manner in which we should engage in conversation. We complete these excessive preparations due to our fear of being judged or humiliated—even though there is no evidence this will occur. Finally, after hours of agonising, we give in to the fear, stay home on a Friday evening, and watch Netflix by ourselves with a large tub of ice cream!

In the case of social anxiety, we assume that others think negatively about us by default. With my patients, I challenge them gently:

"Are you a mind reader?" The answer is "No."

"Are you God?" The answer is "No."

"Are you all-knowing?" The answer is "No."

"So, how do you know that they are thinking about you in a certain way? You don't live inside their heads." And the penny drops.

The first step towards overcoming our persistent thoughts is to accept that thoughts are just thoughts. Thoughts are not reality!

2. Thoughts Only Become Reality When We Act on Them

Thoughts are ideas which exist inside our minds. They need our actions to become reality. In other words, reality is thought that has been actualised by our behaviour. This account in Genesis 4:1-8 illustrates the point:

> Adam made love to his wife Eve, and she became pregnant and gave birth to Cain. She said, "With the help of the Lord I have brought forth a man." Later she gave birth to his brother Abel.
>
> Now Abel kept flocks, and Cain worked the soil. In the course of time Cain brought some of the fruits of the soil as an offering to the Lord. And Abel also brought an offering—fat portions from some of the firstborn of his flock. The Lord looked with favour on Abel and his offering, but on Cain and his offering he did not look with favour. So, Cain was very angry, and his face was downcast.
>
> Then the Lord said to Cain, "Why are you angry? Why is your face

downcast? If you do what is right, will you not be accepted? But if you
do not do what is right, sin is crouching at your door; it desires to have
you, but you must rule over it."
Now Cain said to his brother Abel, "Let's go out to the field." While
they were in the field, Cain attacked his brother Abel and killed him.

Cain was angry with his brother because the Lord had accepted Abel's offering but not Cain's. He harboured angry thoughts towards Abel, and put in motion a plan to kill him by suggesting that they go out to the field away from home. There, he killed Abel in a premeditated manner. He thought about it, he dwelt on it, he planned it, and he did it!

Notice the Lord's warning to Cain:

But if you do not do what is right, sin is crouching at your door; it
desires to have you, but you must rule over it.

— VERSE 7

The reality of the sin of murder had not yet happened when God spoke to Cain. In fact, Cain's murderous intentions towards Abel would not have become a reality if he had overcome his thoughts and chosen not to act on them.

3. It is Easier to Let a Thought Pass than to Stop It

Have you ever heard the lesson about thoughts and the pink elephant? This exercise explores the concept of mental imagery and the limitations of trying to suppress certain thoughts. If we are told *not* to think about a pink elephant, our mind will voluntarily conjure up the image of a pink elephant—despite our strenuous efforts to suppress it. In reminding ourselves to stop thinking about the pink elephant, our mind also reinforces its image in our mind, making it less likely that we will stop thinking about it. This lesson highlights the power of our thoughts and proves that simply trying to control them by willpower can be counterproductive. It is easier to let a thought pass than to suppress it. It is also more beneficial to focus on positive and constructive thoughts than negative ones. In fact, fixating on negative thoughts will just give more "life" to those thoughts. Eventually, they will become autonomous, popping into our minds whether we want them there or not.

4. We Are More than the Sum of Our Thoughts

When a person finds themselves in an anxious situation, it is very easy to be dominated by anxious and worrying thoughts. These thoughts become more and more "sticky" as the domination grows. Eventually, they become an obsession and the person loses their sense of true being. The obsession now grows unhindered, gradually taking over more and more of their life as though the person's entire existence is defined by the obsession. This is usually when the diagnosis of obsessive compulsive disorder is made by a psychiatrist.

Many Christians who suffer from anxious thoughts develop obsessive compulsive disorder of a religious kind. The initial trigger is usually a certain fearful thought of behaving wrongly or perpetrating some sinful act. The Christian feels very guilty about having the thought and attempts to rid themselves of it. But as we've learned with the pink elephant, the more a person tries to get rid of a thought, the more that thought hangs around, keeping the person in a constant hyperarousal state of fight-flight. By this time, the thought becomes an obsession—it no longer shows up based on whether or not the person was thinking about it. The obsession is now autonomous and independent of the thinker. This is called rumination.

At this stage, shame replaces guilt. The Christian hides his or her struggles from those who could help. In some severe cases, fellowship with believers may be severed—the shame is so severe that they cannot reconcile how the obsession could co-exist with their Christian faith. Paradoxically, a pastor is the last person the Christian would want to speak to for fear of condemnation.

The reality is that we are more than our thoughts and the sum of all our thoughts. Psalm 139:13-18 says:

For you created my inmost being; you knit me together in my mother's womb. I praise you because I am fearfully and wonderfully made; your works are wonderful, I know that full well. My frame was not hidden from you when I was made in the secret place, when I was woven together in the depths of the earth. Your eyes saw my unformed body; all the days ordained for me were written in your book before one of them came to be. How precious to me are your thoughts, God! How vast is the sum of them! Were I to count them, they would outnumber the grains of sand—when I awake, I am still with you.

We cannot define ourselves by our thoughts alone!

DEALING WITH OUR ANXIOUS THOUGHTS BY ANCHORING

Have you ever been deep-sea fishing? I have, many times, and I can tell you it is a very exciting sport—when you catch some fish. But when you return home empty-handed, it all feels most frustrating! Imagine now you are out deep-sea fishing and you find a spot where the fish seem eager to take your bait. You are most exhilarated, and you anticipate a big harvest. But the swell is large, and your boat is drifting, so to keep your boat steady and prevent it from drifting away from the promising fishing grounds, you drop an anchor into the seabed. Now your boat holds fast to one place. It will not be tossed to and fro on the water.

The idea of *Anchoring* our mind is precisely the same. It is "the ability to fasten oneself to rational thoughts, biblical truths or positive past experiences, to counter the worrying thoughts which accompany fearful and anxious feelings".

When we are beset with anxious feelings or fears, which commonly come in the form of waves, we need to drop something into our conscious awareness so that our minds will not drift to negative or catastrophic scenarios. Whatever we drop into our consciousness will become the focus of our attention, overriding the negative and pessimistic thoughts that may try to distract us.

In the midst of the storm of our fight-flight response, we can 'drop anchor' by fastening our minds to a rational thought, a past successful experience over our anxiety and fear, a biblical truth or verse which calms our spirit, a promise of God which brings a peaceful feeling, or a statement of self-encouragement.

Anchoring is an exercise which is sadly seldom taught amongst Christians, yet it can be so beneficial, even for those who do not experience panic attacks or suffer from anxiety disorders. I use it frequently myself, as it is a useful tool for stress management and to promote spiritual growth. I also practice *Anchoring* as a form of Christian meditation and to "take captive every thought to make it obedient to Christ" (2 Corinthians 10:4-5). But for those who suffer with acute or chronic anxiety, *Anchoring* is especially helpful.

Anchoring in Acute Anxiety

During an attack of acute anxiety, our body physiology and our thoughts are quickly overtaken by the fight-flight response. Our perception is one of danger, irrespective of the actual environment. *Anchoring* in the midst of acute anxiety involves the following steps:

1. Acknowledge the bodily sensations of anxiety without judgement (refer to Chapter 9: Be Aware) and label your emotions (e.g. "I am feeling anxious.")

2. Register the anxious thoughts without elaboration, saying to yourself, "These are anxious thoughts."

3. If you are sitting, standing or lying down, feel the weight of your body parts against a physical surface, e.g. your feet on the floor, your legs against a chair, your back on a bed. Say to yourself, "I am sitting/standing/lying here in (name the place you are in, e.g. church, a shopping centre, home)," and continue with, "I am safe" or "I am okay."

4. Don't be in a hurry; stay and linger on the *Anchoring* exercise and repeat the statements to yourself for as long as it takes the mind and body to slow down.

5. Reinforce your *Anchoring* with a Bible verse. Recite it aloud to

yourself to immerse your spirit in its truth. Two verses I teach my patients to recite are:

When you pass through the waters, I will be with you; and when you pass through the rivers, they will not sweep over you. When you walk through the fire, you will not be burned; the flames will not set you ablaze.

— *ISAIAH 43:2*

Peace I leave with you; my peace I give you. I do not give to you as the world gives. Do not let your hearts be troubled and do not be afraid.

— *JOHN 14:27*

The steps I have outlined above start with *Anchoring* your physical sensations first; finding stillness and firmness as your body comes into contact with the floor or a chair. This counteracts the sensation of motion sickness and dizziness often generated by the fight-flight hormones during a panic attack.

Once your body is anchored, you can then reinforce this by *Anchoring* your mind, choosing a method which best gives you a sense of peace. The majority of my patients, both Christians and even some non-Christians, find the short verse of John 14:27 very helpful. This passage speaks of Jesus imparting peace, and they can purposely visualise Him stretching out His hand to bless them with peace.

You can find many more verses in the Bible with which to anchor in times of anxiety or distress. Simply type in phrases such as "Do not worry" or "Fear not" in a Bible app, and numerous verses will pop up. Pick one prayerfully which resonates with your personality. For example, most of my patients like Isaiah 43:2 because it depicts a scene of adversity, much like an anxiety attack. Others prefer a verse which is less intense, such as Isaiah 41:10:

So do not fear, for I am with you; do not be dismayed, for I am your God. I will strengthen you and help you; I will uphold you with my righteous right hand.

~

Last but not least, *Anchoring* takes practice. And remember to keep on practising even when your anxiety attacks have settled down. Sadly, most of us don't do that once we've assuaged a bout of anxiety. But I often encourage my patients, "The best time to learn how to swim is not when you are drowning!" Many of us stop *Anchoring* when we reach a temporary reprieve, only to find that the anxiety attacks return later and catch us unprepared. I often draw an analogy with my old Toyota Corolla which I owned as a poor medical student many years ago. One day, the radiator overheated to the extent that I needed to pull the car off the road to let it cool down. It settled after that event, but the radiator would still overheat randomly. I got into the habit of carrying a bottle of water in the car and routinely checking the heat levels. That way, if it looked like we were in for a repeat incident, I could stop it before it really got started. Our nervous system is just like my wonky radiator. Sometimes the fear response kicks in, even when there is no evidence of external danger.

Anchoring in Chronic Anxiety

People who suffer from chronic anxiety disorders tend to have anxious thoughts rumbling in the background like an annoying toothache. These are usually identified by the sufferers as worries, and they are less overwhelming than the blaring anxious thoughts of a panic attack. But non-stop worries still rob a person of freedom and joy in life.

Thoughts associated with chronic anxiety disorders usually carry the themes of lack of competence or a lack of security.

The *Anchoring* exercise for overcoming chronically anxious thoughts involves:

- Recognise the bodily sensations of anxiety without judgement (refer to Chapter 9: Be Aware).
- Acknowledge the anxious thoughts by saying, "This is an anxious thought."

- Anchor your mind to a successful experience in the past, e.g. "I have been in this situation before and I did fine" or "I have done this many times before and the outcome was positive."
- Anchor your mind with a biblical promise or truth about yourself. Refer to the following Scriptures:

I can do all this through him who gives me strength.
— PHILIPPIANS 4:13

Whoever dwells in the shelter of the Most High will rest in the shadow of the Almighty. I will say of the Lord, "He is my refuge and my fortress, my God, in whom I trust."
— PSALM 91:1-2

For the Spirit God gave us does not make us timid, but gives us power, love and self-discipline.
— 2 TIMOTHY 1:7

You may have your own favourite verses that speak of security and confidence to use for *Anchoring*.

- In the mind of your spirit, see yourself going about your daily routine fully anchored in the truth of a Bible verse that speaks of strength and peace, or place yourself in the imagery of the shelter of the Most High over you (Psalm 91:1-2).
- As you go about your daily routine, be consciously aware of your thoughts and self-talk. If there is any hint of an anxious thought or anxious self-talk, do not debate with it nor engage it in any form. Instead, gently recall the *Anchoring* statement, imagery, Bible truth, or promise you have focused on earlier in the day.
- End your day by doing another *Anchoring* exercise before bedtime. Note any success you have had over any anxiety problems during the day. Linger in that feeling of success. Express your gratitude to God. Congratulate yourself!

Remember the event of this success and save it for *Anchoring* yourself another day.

~

When you practice something often, such as exercise and going to the gym, it becomes a part of your lifestyle. *Anchoring* enhances our mental health, and it makes us less susceptible to stress and anxiety. I highly recommend it to you for your own mental and spiritual health.

11

Be Still and Know

The previous two exercises, *Be Aware* and *Anchoring,* lead naturally to this third exercise: *Be Still and Know.* To recap, the *Be Aware* exercise helps in recognising and accepting anxious feelings without judgement and interpretation, as these send us into a tailspin, creating chaos. That chaos escalates our anxiety and fear and compounds the fight-flight response. And it is the latter response which exacerbates the outpouring of stress hormones, heightens our vigilance, and promotes avoidance and withdrawal behaviours. The *Anchoring* exercise further helps the mind to de-focus on negative and anxious thoughts. It disentangles the mind from the enmeshment of obsessive thoughts and prevents those obsessive thoughts from becoming automatic negative thoughts which run on their own beyond our volitional control. *Anchoring* frees up our mind space so that we can meaningfully and positively deal with our fear and anxiety.

The *Be Still and Know* exercise is a journey into the inner sanctum of one's being—a pilgrimage to the core of our spirit. It is an exercise which removes the battle from our mind and brings it into the peace and quiet of our spirit. I have treated many Christians who suffer from chronic fear and anxiety. They have been to various therapists to seek counselling for their fear and anxiety, but their improvement has been limited. Some are also on psychotropic medications, and invariably they have a chaotic and restless mind. They try to take their thoughts captive, as 2 Corinthians 10:5 describes:

> We demolish arguments and every pretension that sets itself up against the knowledge of God, and we take captive every thought to make it obedient to Christ.

But their mind is often so chaotic that they cannot focus. Some say that what they believe in their minds has no effect on their state of being. Others have experienced another voice in their mind, arguing what is contrary to their correct beliefs. These individuals have experienced trauma to such an extent their mind is trapped in a state of hypervigilance. They can't focus because their mind is constantly scanning for danger and threats which no longer exist. Rather than simply teaching them to analyse whether their thoughts are logical, or telling them to try not to think about it (the pink elephant approach!), I have learnt that a more beneficial approach is to teach them the exercise of *Be still and Know*.

THE 'BE STILL AND KNOW' EXERCISE

Be Still and Know is an exercise rooted in Christian spirituality. For me, to be still is to assume a spiritual posture of trust, patience, and yielding. It is a cessation from striving and fighting, which makes it the perfect antidote for the flight-fight posture one tends to adopt when confronted with perceived danger. On a physiological level, *Be Still and Know* neutralises the hypervigilance and hyperarousal of the adrenal state that has been brought about by fear and anxiety. In the Bible, there are a number of passages which mention the idea of being still. These include:

> *Be still before the Lord and wait patiently for him; do not fret when people succeed in their ways, when they carry out their wicked schemes.*
>
> — PSALM 37:7

> *The Lord will fight for you; you need only to be still.*
>
> — EXODUS 14:14

Be still, and know that I am God; I will be exalted among the nations,
I will be exalted in the earth.

— PSALM 46:10

Let us now go a bit deeper to truly understand this spiritual posture, by looking more closely at Exodus chapter 14.

The story begins with the Israelites, descendants of Jacob, who had settled in Egypt during a time of famine. Initially, they were welcomed by the Egyptians, but they eventually found themselves enslaved and oppressed by a new Pharaoh who feared their growing numbers. The Israelites were ill-treated by Pharoah, and they cried out to God for deliverance. Eventually, God raised up a deliverer in the person of Moses—a Hebrew who became an Egyptian prince when he was adopted by Pharaoh's daughter and raised in Pharaoh's court.

After personally encountering God in a burning bush, Moses confronted Pharaoh with God's demand to let His people go. When Pharaoh refused, a series of ten plagues were sent upon Egypt, culminating in the final and most devastating plague which was the death of the firstborn of every Egyptian household. Moses was instructed to tell Pharaoh that he must let the Israelites go so that they might worship God, because they were His firstborn (Exodus 4:22-23). Following the death of his own firstborn, Pharaoh finally relented and let the Israelites go. But he soon regretted his decision. He gathered his army and chariots and pursued the Israelites into the wilderness, and it is at this point that the narrative of Exodus 14 begins.

The Israelites soon found themselves trapped in the wilderness, with Pharaoh's army behind them and the Red Sea in front of them. With nowhere to go, the Israelites were greatly terrified. At the thought of being slaughtered by Pharoah's army, they turned their terror into rage. They complained bitterly to Moses that they would rather be enslaved in Egypt than die in the wilderness (Exodus 14:10-12). Moses responded:

Do not be afraid. Stand firm and you will see the deliverance the Lord will bring you today. The Egyptians you see today you will never see again. The Lord will fight for you; you need only to be still.

— EXODUS 14:13-14

The Lord said to Moses:

Why are you crying out to me? Tell the Israelites to move on. Raise your staff and stretch out your hand over the sea to divide the water so that the Israelites can go through the sea on dry ground. I will harden the hearts of the Egyptians so that they will go in after them. And I will gain glory through Pharaoh and all his army, through his chariots and his horsemen. The Egyptians will know that I am the Lord when I gain glory through Pharaoh, his chariots and his horsemen.

— EXODUS 14:15-18

There are two parts to the spiritual exercise of *Be Still and Know*. The first part is to simply be still. The second part is to "know" and engage with God in a very personal and proactive way. "Being still" is not passively relinquishing oneself to fate or karma. It is not avoidance or withdrawal, and it is not detaching oneself from reality and one's environment or retreating into one's imagination or fantasy. It is not the "emptying of one's mind". *Be Still and Know* is holding an active awareness of one's fear and anxiety, but also knowingly engaging with God and being convinced and convicted that things will be different because of His presence. The stillness helps us to override the flight-fight hormone, to disengage from our primitive instinct of fear of annihilation, and to engage with our personal God. But stillness without knowing is pointless. No matter the circumstance, we must learn to turn towards and engage with our Lord and Saviour.

The confidence that I have from being still is not based on some mystical, New Age spirituality, but on my knowledge of a covenantal God with whom I have an intimate and loving relationship. This is shown in a very well-known verse in the Bible:

*He says, "Be still, and know that I am God; I will be exalted among
the nations, I will be exalted in the earth."*

— PSALM 46:10

COVENANTAL RELATIONSHIP IS THE BASIS OF KNOWING

Let us examine a bit more closely the idea of knowing God and this
covenantal relationship.

In the Old Testament of the Bible, the Hebrew word for "know" is
"yada". This word carries a deeper and more intimate connotation than
mere intellectual knowledge. In the English language, the word "know"
often means an intellectual understanding. Some examples are "I know
German," "I know how to roast a delicious turkey," or "I know astronomy,"
etc. Sometimes, when it comes to knowledge about a person, we might
specify, "I know him well." In other words, we imply that our knowledge
about him is deeper than most people's, and our knowledge is not confined
to the superficial but extends into personal knowing. But "yada" is even
deeper than that. It signifies a profound, experiential knowledge, including
personal relationships and understanding.

Adam and Eve's Covenantal Relationship

Let us look at the relationship between Adam and Eve, which is the
prototypic "yada" relationship. Adam and Eve have a relationship that is
characterised by a deep intimacy and profound connection. They are so
connected that they are described in Genesis 2:23 and 24 as one:

*The man said, "This is now bone of my bones and flesh of my flesh; she
shall be called 'woman', for she was taken out of man." That is why a
man leaves his father and mother and is united to his wife, and they
become one flesh.*

Later in Genesis 4:1 we read:

Now Adam knew Eve his wife, and she conceived and bore Cain. (NKJV)

Adam's knowing of Eve was more than just a physical and sexual relationship. It was an intimacy of the spirit, soul, and body. Such intimacy involves the entire person's being.

Our Covenantal Relationship with God

Our "yada" relationship with God is also not based on mere intellectual understanding or theology. It is one of deep experiential connection. It is more than a matter of the head; it is a matter of the heart. Such a relationship means personally experiencing the personhood of God and His attributes of love, mercy, faithfulness, justice, and holiness.

The Old Testament

In the Old Testament, a number of well-known Bible characters have a covenantal relationship with God. These include Moses, who was called by God to lead the children of Israel out of Egypt's slavery and into the Promised Land. Through Moses, the Ten Commandments were given to the children of Israel. In fact, Moses was so close to God that he asked to see His glory face to face (Exodus 33:18-23).

Another person worth mentioning is Abraham whose relationship with God is based on the Abrahamic Covenant (Genesis 12:1-3). This relationship is characterised by Abraham trusting and believing that God was faithful and would deliver whatever He promised (Hebrews 11:8-12). Abraham had such an intimate relationship with God that he was later described as the "friend of God" (James 2:23).

King David is yet another Old Testament character who experienced God in a very intimate way. David wrote many Psalms where he poured his heart out to God. His writings flowed out of his intimate relationship with God whom he trusts and obeys. One of the most beautiful Psalms that David wrote is Psalm 23, in which David depicts God as the gentle, protective, caring, and gracious shepherd. David intimately knew the heart of God, and this is even written in 1 Samuel 13:14:

But now your kingdom will not endure; the Lord has sought out a man after his own heart and appointed him ruler of his people, because you have not kept the Lord's command.

In this passage, the prophet Samuel is speaking to King Saul, telling him that God has chosen a new future leader for His people—a man after His own heart. This man is none other than David, who later becomes King David, known for his deep relationship with God.

The New Testament

Jeremiah 31:31-34 foretells the extraordinary promise of God in establishing the New Covenant:

"The days are coming," declares the Lord, "when I will make a new covenant . . . I will put my law in their minds and write it on their hearts. I will be their God, and they will be my people. No longer will they teach their neighbour, or say to one another, 'Know the Lord', because they will all know me, from the least of them to the greatest," declares the Lord. "For I will forgive their wickedness and will remember their sins no more."

What a powerful promise! And we now know that Jesus is the fulfilment of the New Covenant. This is why He said in Luke 22:20:

This cup is the new covenant in my blood, which is poured out for you.

Through Jesus' work and His death on the Cross, He has made it possible for us to come into a new and intimate relationship with God (John 14:6, John 1:12). Due to the atoning sacrifice of Christ on the cross, we now have a "yada" relationship with God the Father. Jesus Christ described this intimacy and connection with God in John 17:21-23:

. . . Father, just as you are in me, and I am in you. May they also be in us so that the world may believe that you have sent me. I have given them the glory that you gave me, that they may be one as we are one—I in them and you in me—so that they may be brought to

complete unity. Then the world will know that you sent me and have loved them even as you have loved me.

The intimacy we have with God is made possible by our identification with Christ. That is why the Apostle Paul declared in Romans 8:14-17:

For those who are led by the Spirit of God are the children of God. The Spirit you received does not make you slaves, so that you live in fear again; rather, the Spirit you received brought about your adoption to sonship. And by him we cry, "Abba, Father." The Spirit himself testifies with our spirit that we are God's children. Now if we are children, then we are heirs—heirs of God and co-heirs with Christ.

We know God as our "Abba" (our personally intimate father), just as Jesus knows His Father as Abba (John 20:17).

This is our "yada" relationship with God. It is a deep connection based on the finished work of Christ on the cross of Calvary! God also desires us to have this "yada" relationship with him. For those who deal with anxiety, this beautiful promise is a reminder that God Himself longs for us to feel safe in relationship with Him.

BEING STILL AND KNOWING IS MOVING
INTO THE SPIRITUAL REALM

Christian inner healing enables us to move from dealing with the somatic experience to dealing with the mind and then with one's spirit. It is a journey from the outer (body), to the inner (the mind), and then to the innermost (the spirit). It takes time to cultivate the spiritual exercise of *Being Still* and *Knowing*. Immersing one's spirit in the biblical narrative helps a Christian adopt this spiritual posture of being still and knowing. Let's look again at the account in Exodus 14:13-14:

Moses answered the people, "Do not be afraid. Stand firm and you will see the deliverance the Lord will bring you today. The Egyptians

you see today you will never see again. The Lord will fight for you;
you need only to be still."

In this case, the Egyptian army was in hot pursuit of the children of Israel who had just escaped generations of slavery. The Red Sea lay in front of them, and the army was fast approaching from behind. Notice that Moses' command to the Israelites is the exact spiritual posture we need to adopt in the face of anxiety and fear:

1. Do Not Be Afraid

Despite the surge of the flight-fight hormones on our bodies, and with all the discomfort that comes with that, we can choose not to react. Reacting would only escalate the stress response and perpetuate the anxiety and fear. We merely need to acknowledge intellectually that this is a situation of fear and anxiety, but then choose to anchor ourselves in biblical truth and maintain the posture of being still and knowing God, who is in control (Isaiah 46:9-10).

2. Stand Firm

Having dealt with our emotions of fear and anxiety, we now turn to our will. We are commanded to stand firm, but what does this mean? The command of standing firm appears numerous times throughout the Bible. It is a position that believers are told to assume in times of battle and warfare:

> *You will not have to fight this battle. Take up your positions; stand firm*
> *and see the deliverance the Lord will give you, Judah and Jerusalem.*
> *Do not be afraid; do not be discouraged. Go out to face them tomorrow,*
> *and the Lord will be with you.*
>
> — 2 CHRONICLES 20:17

The Apostle Paul frequently admonished Christians to "stand firm" in his various Epistles; for example he exhorts this in 1 Corinthians 15:58 and 16:13, 2 Corinthians 1:21 and 24, Philippians 4:1 and Colossians 4:12. The most notable speech Paul gives regarding this mantra is found in Ephesians 6:14:

Stand firm then, with the belt of truth buckled around your waist, with the breastplate of righteousness in place.

In this context, "standing firm" means remaining unwavering in one's faith, convictions, and righteousness, in the face of spiritual battles and challenges. It implies being resolute and unshaken in one's commitment to living according to God's truth and righteousness. Just as a soldier stands firm and ready in battle, believers are called to stand firm in their faith and in their adherence to God's principles, relying on the spiritual armour provided by God for protection and strength.

3. Expecting Deliverance

It is hard to have positive expectations when we are gripped with fear and anxiety. But expecting deliverance is precisely what we need. Unless we have that hope, we will most likely flee as soon as we are struck with an anxiety attack or fear. However, for those who have been experiencing chronic anxiety and fear, they have come many times to a place of giving up—a passive acceptance that there is nothing they can do, and that even if there *were* something they could do, nothing would change anyway. This was precisely the experience of a patient of mine, who came under my care a few years ago. I will identify him as Brayden Thomas (not his real name).

CASE STUDY

Brayden Thomas (Chronic Anxiety Disorder)

Brayden was twenty-eight years old when he was first referred to me. Having suffered from a chronic anxiety disorder since his early childhood, Brayden remembered being anxious for most of his life. He felt stressed about almost all situations in life, no matter how many times he had experienced similar situations before. "For some reason, my brain would just tell me that this time it's different; this time something bad will happen," he told me. Brayden had sought help from a number of counsellors, psychiatrists, and psychologists before he was referred to me. He had been taught cognitive behavioural therapy but he had found it unhelpful. In fact, the therapy had caused him more distress and increased his feeling of hopelessness because, even after identifying his irrational thoughts and correcting them, he remained anxious.

I taught Brayden the steps of *Be Aware* and *Anchoring*, helping him to note his anxiety without reacting and then to anchor on an experience which gave him positive emotions and could hold him firm despite the anxiety swirling around him. He was making good progress until we came to the step of expecting deliverance. After struggling with anxiety for over twenty years and experiencing defeat again and again despite seeing a number of professionals, it was difficult for Brayden to anticipate deliverance. His therapy came to an impasse that could not be resolved until he could accept that this step involved engaging with his beliefs, but without him actively doing anything. Just like Brayden, a lot of people find it difficult when they don't have to *do* anything to fix their problems of anxiety and fear. Just believing at this point that it will be fixed seems too good to be true. Then one day, Brayden arrived at his session in an upbeat mood. He told me he'd had a breakthrough and had managed to arrive at the point of expecting deliverance from God in his struggle with chronic anxiety. He had reached this place simply by asking himself, "What is the one thing that is harder to believe than the belief that I could receive deliverance from God?" His answer was simple: the forgiveness of his sins when he first became a Christian. And with that, Brayden managed to move on in his journey to overcoming his chronic anxiety.

Much has been written about the power of positive expectation, including articles on positive psychology, the power of positive thinking, and metaphysical beliefs discussing how we can shape the universe by our internal thoughts. On a physiological level at least, we know that positive expectation induces the release of neurochemicals such as dopamine and endorphins which directly oppose the flight-fight effects of the stress hormones. And for Christians, positive expectation is the outworking of faith which is so beautifully articulated in the book of Hebrews chapter eleven.

MENTAL HEALTH IN SEARCH OF SPIRITUALITY

4. Raising Your Hand

At the terrifying impasse beside the Red Sea, Moses was commanded to raise his hand over the waters. Some years ago, I watched a re-run of the 1956 movie "The Ten Commandments" produced by Cecil B DeMille. The scene showed Moses stretching out his hand. Immediately the Red Sea parted, and the children of Israel walked across the dry seabed to the other side, escaping the Egyptian army. But the Exodus narrative recorded something quite different:

> *Then Moses stretched out his hand over the sea, and all that night the Lord drove the sea back with a strong east wind and turned it into dry land. The waters were divided.*
>
> — EXODUS 14:21

It seems that Moses stretched out his hand over the sea for quite some time, during which God parted the sea with a strong east wind. This is similar to the account of Moses raising his hands in prayer on the hill whilst Joshua fought the Amalekites. As long as Moses' hands remained raised, Joshua's army would prevail (Exodus 17:8-13).

Let us consider the significance of the raised hand. From a spiritual perspective, people in prayer with raised hands usually signifies a desire to connect with and receive a blessing from God. But in the context of the Exodus account, it also signified a partnership with God, albeit in a minor way, to accomplish what He had planned.

To put it simply, raising our hand in a struggle with anxiety and fear means we want to listen to God, remain connected to Him, and partner with Him in overcoming our fear and anxiety by being yoked with Him. Whenever we do this, our fruitless striving stops. We are no longer entangled in our fear and anxiety because we are connected to Him.

In conclusion, *Be Still and Know* is an exercise of the heart. It is a spiritual posture based on our intimate relationship with God, and it transcends intellectual knowledge and rational debate. It is a position of rest due to a deep assurance that God is in control and He will prevail. And as we are intimately connected to Him, we can "know" that His victory is our victory. We are overcomers because He has overcome it all. In dealing with our fear and anxiety, *Be Still and Know* moves us from the skills of *Be Aware* (where we accurately appraise our bodily sensations without judgement) and *Anchoring* (where we deal with the thoughts in our mind) to finding peace in our heart and spirit.

12

The Presence

Adopting a spiritual posture of *being still and knowing* is a prelude to the next stage of the spiritual exercise of entering into His presence.

We adopt a spiritual posture of stillness in anticipation that God will reveal Himself and His work in our lives. His revelation of Himself is His presence. Have you ever had a moment in your life when you can sense the presence of God so tangibly and knowingly in your spirit? Many times, I have sensed the presence of God, often when I have stepped into Christian meetings. Such an experience is beyond intellectual understanding. The meeting place is the same, the same musicians play the same familiar songs, and the people who sit in the pews are the same people. But deep inside my spirit, I perceive that His presence is so tangible it is as though I have stepped into another dimension.

I have experienced a number of times when the presence of God has left an indelible mark on my spirit. I did not seek the presence of God; it just happened to me like a visitation from God. One such experience occurred when I was baptised at the age of fourteen. Like many Asians of Chinese ancestry, I was born into a Buddhist family. My baptism was therefore a very significant event in my life, as it was not one of my family traditions but a public demonstration of a change in my faith. I was baptised by immersion, and no—nothing extraordinary happened when I emerged out of the water. But for many days after my baptism, I felt as though the presence of God had enveloped me. It was a warm feeling in my spirit, and I felt loved and special. The world around me was a beautiful place, and I had a deep sense of wellbeing. I did not have the words to describe it then, but looking back, perhaps that is the "shalom" which is so central to the Judeo-Christian faith. Shalom is a deep sense of completeness, wholeness, wellbeing, and harmony.

Another occasion in which I sensed God's presence occurred around the time I sat for my specialist Fellowship examination. In Australia, a doctor cannot become a medical specialist until they complete at least five years of study and training. This culminates in a series of examinations which ends with a face-to-face appraisal. I had just reached that final phase. Passing meant I would be admitted to the Royal College and be recognised as a consultant psychiatrist, but that final assessment is notoriously arduous. The pass rate is low, sometimes only 50%. Most candidates do not pass the first time, and it is not unusual for many to attempt and fail the examination repeatedly, only to finally quit and become a general practitioner.

Like many doctors who seek to specialise, after a long journey of undergraduate studies and more years of learning as a trainee specialist, I was already married and expecting the birth of my first child. The stakes for me were high, and I had a conversation with God: "Father, I have studied so hard and done everything I could. I have only given myself one shot to pass, as I can't afford to keep going if I fail. I want to be responsible and raise my family. So if I fail, I will become a general practitioner. It is up to you now, Father!" I also recruited my mother-in-law—a prayer warrior—and her intercessors to pray for me, then I flew to Melbourne for the final examination.

The night before my assessment, I could not sleep. A thousand scenarios flew through my mind of what the examination might be like, and I eventually took a sleeping pill. This made my worries even worse, as I now feared I would sleep through the alarm. I only slept for three hours that night, waking up physically exhausted. But an unusual sensation had settled upon me, as though I was cocooned in a bubble that enveloped my whole being. I felt protected, invincible, and untouchable. It was most extraordinary. I knew it was the presence of God. I survived three clinical vivas with real patients, and another hour of grilling by two professors. The next evening, I was invited to the college dinner to celebrate my success, and I put on my best suit and tie for the occasion. A few weeks after I passed my Fellowship examination, my daughter was born. My life was joy unspeakable.

In the 1950s, a neurosurgeon named Dr. Wilder Penfield studied epilepsy in his patients by stimulating different parts of the brain with electric probes. One day, he stimulated a patient's temporal lobe which is involved in memory formation. His patient immediately "relived" specific events with complete vividness including the five senses and the emotions associated with those memories. It seems all our life experiences are stored in our brains, though we cannot access them easily. Indeed, those who experience near death frequently describe seeing their whole life flash before them like a movie.

These two experiences of sensing God's tangible presence in my life left a significant mark on my spirit. Whenever I step into a state of stillness and prayerfulness and recall these events, my spirit is ushered back to the presence of the Father, as fresh as ever. It is as though there is a spiritual portal through which I can access the presence of God. Like Dr. Wilder's patient who vividly relived their past experience, I believe that when we adopt a spiritual posture of stillness and prayerfulness, we can step back into the presence of God through our memories. After all, He is a timeless God.

THREE BRIDGES INTO THE PRESENCE OF GOD

There are three bridges which help me to step into the presence of God. Let me share them with you:

1. Your Personal Memorial

In the Bible, a *memorial* is often a physical object, ceremony, or practice established to commemorate a significant event or covenant with God. It reminds us of God's faithfulness, His miraculous interventions, or His fulfilment of promises. In turn, we return to Him our gratitude, reverence, and worship.

We can read about the *memorial* in Jacob's life in Genesis 28:10-22. Jacob was running away from his brother Esau who wanted to kill him, and he came to a point where he was so exhausted that he fell asleep on the ground. As he slept, he dreamt of a ladder reaching from heaven to earth, with angels walking up and down the ladder. Then in his dream, God spoke, reaffirming the Abraham covenant to Jacob. When Jacob woke up, he acknowledged God as his God. Then he set up a *memorial* using a stone and called the place Bethel, which means the house of God.

Many years later, in Genesis 35:1-15, we find Jacob on his way to meet Esau in the hopes of offering peace. On the journey, he returned to Bethel where God appeared to Jacob and reaffirmed His covenant again. Jacob set up another stone *memorial* and called the place El-Bethel which means The God of Bethel. On both occasions, Jacob had felt the tangible presence of God, but on this occasion, his faith in God became that much more personal and real. Such is the effect of God, that each time we step into His presence, our life changes and He becomes even more personally known to us.

For Christians, a *memorial* which is common to us is the Lord's Supper or Communion. Instituted by Jesus Christ Himself, the first Communion is recorded in the first three Gospels of the Bible. Jesus used bread and wine as a symbol of His body, broken for our sins, and His blood, shed for our sins (Luke 22:19-20). The elements of the Lord's Supper are a reminder of the New Covenant into which He has entered with all believers. Essentially, Communion is a *memorial* for Christians.

I consider the two personal experiences I shared as a type of *memorial* for me. They remind me of the presence of God and His love and faithfulness in my life. They are not as dramatic as Jacob's experiences, but God works differently in each of our lives. Do you have an experience of a very close encounter with God and His presence? That is your bridge to His presence.

Remember, a *memorial* is a personal and positive testimony of God's presence and goodness manifested in your life. A memorial can lead you into the presence of God as you follow these steps:

1. Adopt a spiritual posture of *being still and knowing* (refer to Chapter 11).

2. Slowly recall the scene from your past, and think on sound, touch, or other sensory stimuli which are associated with the *memorial* experience.
3. Allow your spirit to bring back the full memory to your mind. Slowly build up the details of the *memorial* experience as you fill in the gaps.
4. When your spirit has filled in the details, go deep within yourself. Allow your spirit to tarry in the presence of God.

2. Your Safe Place

Without thinking too hard about the answer, I'd like you to consider this question: "What aspect of Jesus' life (as recorded in the Gospels) most stands out to you?" Is it His miracles? His parables? His clever discourse with the Pharisees and Sadducees?

I wonder how many of us say, "His retreat to the mountain"?

There are numerous records of Jesus going up into the mountains to pray to His Father.

After he had dismissed them, he went up on a mountainside by himself to pray. Later that night, he was there alone . . .

— MATTHEW 14:23

After leaving them, he went up on a mountainside to pray.

— MARK 6:46

One of those days Jesus went out to a mountainside to pray and spent the night praying to God.

— LUKE 6:12

About eight days after Jesus said this, he took Peter, John and James with him and went up onto a mountain to pray.

— LUKE 9:28

The mountain served as a secluded location where Jesus could engage in intimate communication with His Father, seeking guidance, strength, and spiritual renewal. It was safe from the distraction of the masses, the harassment of His opponents, and even His endless services to the needy. It was a place between Him and His Father. A place of singular focus and immersion in the presence of God. On one of these occasions, as He dwelt in God's presence, Jesus' face became radiant, and His garment shone with dazzling light.

As he was praying, the appearance of his face changed, and his clothes became as bright as a flash of lightning.

— *LUKE 9:29*

Bible scholars interpret this event as the transfiguration of Jesus; He lifted the veil of humanity and revealed His divinity. I remember another person in the Bible whose face shone after spending forty days and forty nights on a mountain with God.

Moses was there with the Lord forty days and forty nights without eating bread or drinking water. And he wrote on the tablets the words of the covenant—the Ten Commandments. When Moses came down from Mount Sinai with the two tablets of the covenant law in his hands, he was not aware that his face was radiant because he had spoken with the Lord.

— *EXODUS 34:28-29*

Some years ago, I had the privilege of making a pilgrimage trip to Egypt and Israel, led by a professor at Regent College in Vancouver, which left an indelible mark on my spirit. As we crossed the Sinai Peninsula, I was in awe of going up Mount Sinai. With another friend, I woke at 3 a.m. in the morning and rode a camel across the wilderness in pitch darkness. The only source of light was the stars. I looked heavenward and wondered, "Is this how Abraham felt when God spoke to him about his descendants being as numerous as the stars?" I imagined I was Abraham and felt a tingling in my being.

At the foot of the mountain, we left our camels and hiked up Mount

Sinai on foot. We met other "pilgrims" along the way, but everyone was quiet in a state of focused anticipation. There was no social chit-chat or loud noises, and I oriented my spirit into a state of stillness. I felt a sense of sacred anticipation over what God would reveal to me. It was still dark when I reached the top of the mountain, and I chose a quiet spot to wait for sunrise, immersing myself in a state of reverence and prayerfulness. When the first ray of sunlight pierced through the darkness, it cast a golden hue on the desert rocks. The dark sky soon turned a blushing red, and I felt a strong sense of God's presence as His finger painted the first and only morning on top of Mount Sinai that I would ever experience. My spirit was full as I gave thanks to Him for His presence and glory. This is my *Memorial*, my *Safe Place*, that I go back to many times in my spirit—my narrative of a once-in-a-lifetime spiritual experience lived in reality.

Do you have a *Safe Place* to meet God? It does not have to be very spectacular. Christians often have favourite places to meet God in prayer or to have quiet time. It may be a private room in the house or a place near nature. Going back to these places, either in person or in our mind, often draws us into the presence of God.

Scripture is also a safe place to meet with God. There are many passages in the Bible which have the features and characteristics of a *Safe Place*. For example, Psalm 23 and Psalm 91 are such places.

Psalm 23 is a *Safe Place* because of the presence of the Good Shepherd who looks after His sheep. The Good Shepherd also keeps the sheep from harm and danger, protecting them from enemies.

The "Secret place of the Most High" is a *Safe Place*, because it is where God dwells. In Psalm 91, we read that in this place, we are "safe from all manner of pestilences, harm, disasters, wild beasts, arrows, and plague." In other words, the presence of God is a place of refuge and a fortress for us all.

Accessing Your Scriptural Safe Place

You can enter a *Scriptural Safe Place* by doing the following exercise:

1. Adopt a spiritual posture of being still and knowing (refer to Chapter 11).
2. Read out the Bible passage which you have chosen, e.g. Psalm 23 or Psalm 91.
3. Immerse your spirit in the selected passage. With the Holy Spirit's help, see the *Safe Place* in your mind.
4. Capture the essence of the *Safe Place* in your mind.
5. Allow your spirit to tarry in the *Safe Place* as you enjoy God's Presence.

A *Scriptural Safe Place* provides us access into the presence of God through His Word. But it may lack a sense of personal history which can make it difficult for some of us to access it easily. On the other hand, a *Personal Safe Place* imbued with actual historical experience normally helps to establish a deeper intimacy in His Presence. I use my *Personal Safe Place* more often than a *Scriptural Safe Place*, but both are useful tools for engaging with God's presence.

Accessing Your Personal Safe Space

(NB: It is best to have a person you trust present with you throughout this exercise. For some, this exercise will be more beneficial as an adjunct to therapy.)

1. Adopt a spiritual posture of "Being Still and Knowing".
2. Slowly recall the scene, sound, touch, or other sensory stimuli which are associated with your *Personal Safe Place*.
3. Slowly build up the details of the *Safe Place*, filling in the gaps as your spirit brings information to your mind.
4. When your spirit has filled in the details, go deep within yourself. Allow your spirit to tarry in the presence of God.

When you are ready, ask God to bring to mind the details of a fear or anxiety struggle that you wish to resolve. Holding firmly to the peace that you experience in His presence:

1. Consider the events or situation preceding the anxiety. Where were you when you experienced the fear or anxiety? What were you doing at the time? What brought on the sense of anxiety or fear?

2. Consider your experience of the anxiety attack. What physical sensations did you feel? How would you rate the severity of the anxiety attack or fear? Is it the same, worse, or better than the last time?

3. Consider the way you managed the anxiety attack. How did you respond in the moment to the anxiety attack or fear? Is there anything you could have done differently?

Now, invite Jesus into the situation or event associated with the anxiety attack. What insights can He share with you about the event or situation that preceded or led to the attack? Are there ways Jesus could have helped you to handle the anxiety attack? You might like to journal your experience of "debriefing with Jesus".

Having a *Safe Place* not only helps in the management of our anxiety and fear, but it also nurtures our walk and relationship with Abba Father. A personal *Safe Place* nourishes our spirit and enhances our development as sons and daughters of God.

But there is another good spiritual exercise which has to do with that moment-to-moment entrance into His Presence. It is not linked with a *Memorial*—which is anchored in a personal memory of His presence and goodness—nor a *Safe Place*—which links a certain place with His presence. Rather, it invites a spiritual dimension into our daily existence as we go about our earthly and seemingly mundane activities. I call this the *Spiritual Space*.

3. Your Spiritual Space

Christians believe that God created the universe (Genesis 1 and 2). He also created time and space. The idea of physical space is well known because we live in and interact with it. We are aware of our physical space because we have a physical body which delineates where we are in relation to others. But we also have a spirit through which we have life (Genesis 2:7). We are both physical and spiritual, yet we pay far less attention to our *Spiritual Space* than our physical space. So what is a *Spiritual Space*?

Spiritual Space refers to a dimension beyond the physical world. It involves connection with our Father God, exploration of our relationship with Him, the understanding of truth, and the search for personal meaning and purpose in life. It may include practices such as prayer, meditation, worship, music, reflection, and contemplation to increase inner peace and spiritual awareness of the presence of God. On this side of heaven, we cannot fully understand *Spiritual Space* without understanding the relationship between spirituality and physicality.

Spirituality Is Interconnected With Physicality

Applying my belief in the bipartiteness of humankind (a human being is comprised of both body and soul), I believe in the interconnectedness of the spiritual and the physical. Indeed, the Bible says, "the body without the spirit is dead" (James 2:26). James further challenges Christians that we cannot express our spirituality in a vacuum devoid of caring for physicality—both ours and the physical needs of those around us who are hungry and cold (James 2:14-17). James says in chapter 1:27:

> *Religion that God our Father accepts as pure and faultless is this: to look after orphans and widows in their distress and to keep oneself from being polluted by the world.*

Jesus also taught extensively on both the physical and spiritual aspects of life, emphasising the interconnectedness of the two. His teachings encompassed various themes related to morality, ethics, salvation, and the nature of reality.

Regarding the physical realm, Jesus emphasised compassion, love, and care for others, especially the marginalised and oppressed. He performed numerous miracles Himself, such as healing the sick (Matthew 14:14), feeding the hungry (Matthew 14:13-21), and even raising the dead (John 11:1-44), demonstrating His power over physical illnesses and death. Consider Jesus' first miracle at the marriage banquet in Cana. It was not driving out evil spirits to demonstrate His spiritual power over darkness but was instead a simple act of turning water into wine. He changed the physical property of the fluid, and even this related to His glory:

> *What Jesus did here in Cana of Galilee was the first of the signs through which he revealed his glory; and his disciples believed in him.*
>
> — JOHN 2:11

Spirituality Is Expressed Through Physicality

The Bible is replete with symbolism of the spiritual being manifested through the physical. From the Tabernacle—and later the Temple—with its furnishing, to the various religious rites, sacrifices and rituals, and the various holy feasts, symbolism abounds. The golden lampstand in both the Tabernacle (Exodus 25:31-40) and the Temple symbolises with its illumination the guidance and wisdom of God in the Old Testament and foreshadows Jesus as the Light of the world (John 8:12). The table of showbread (Exodus 25:23-30) symbolises God as the sustenance of His people and foreshadows Jesus as the Bread of life (John 6:35). And the Feast of the Passover (Exodus 12) foreshadows Jesus as the sacrificial Lamb of God (John 1:29).

During Old Testament times, many of these spiritual activities happened only at a specified time and in a specific physical space which was both corporate and external to oneself. For example, only the high priest could enter the Most Holy Place in the Tabernacle and later the Temple, to offer a yearly sacrifice on the Day of Atonement.

The work of Jesus however has resulted in Christians being a part of the close relationship He has with the Father (John 14:20). There is now unity and interconnectedness between believers and God through Jesus Christ. Through Him, we can experience the presence of God in faith and communion with Jesus. The Apostle Paul echoed this truth when he said that our body is the temple of the Holy Spirit (1 Corinthians 6:19). Spirituality can now be expressed through our personal space. Indeed, we are encouraged to approach God with confidence in the Most Holy Place within our innermost being (Hebrews 4:16).

For me, *Spiritual Space* is very personal. It is a space within myself into which I invite God, so that I may be connected with His presence. It is like Jesus' description in Revelation 3:20:

> *Here I am! I stand at the door and knock. If anyone hears my voice and opens the door, I will come in and eat with that person, and they with me.*

My Spiritual Space

I'd like to share with you how I habitually create a *Spiritual Space* daily, so that I can start my day infused with the presence of God.

Unless it is necessary, I go to sleep without an alarm set for the next day, so that I don't go to sleep with an agenda on my mind. I allow my spirit to wake me at a time not determined by my mind.

When I wake up, I open my eyes slowly instead of jumping out of bed. I allow my spirit to sense the presence of God through my physical sensations or through a thought about God that I recall. This might be a spiritual truth I have learnt, an attribute of God, or a reminiscence of a positive experience. I spend a short time meditating on this.

Next, I direct my attention to my spirit, seeking to capture a sense of peace, containment, and contentment. I get out of bed in a calm fashion, being constantly aware that my Father is with me. By this time, my environment is literally brighter. I allow my spirit to capture any aspects of my environment which reinforce an attribute of God or a truth He has dropped into my heart.

For example, the nice crepe myrtle tree in my back garden may remind me of His beauty. The birds' chirping breaking the silence of the early morning, is a melody worshipping His majesty.

I do fifteen to twenty minutes of physical exercise and prepare my breakfast, all while maintaining a parallel spiritual attention to His presence. Sometimes, I might dialogue with God both verbally and in my spirit. Then I have my breakfast.

After that, I take a moderately long shower, consciously allowing myself to feel the comfort of the water which brings a relaxed feeling. My spirit anticipates that today is a good day that my Father has given me to enjoy and to spend in His will.

I go on to my activities for the day, but I constantly come back to reflect on the truths that my Father has dropped into my spirit during our tranquil greeting of the day together.

So, our journey in managing anxiety and fear involves:

1. Recognising and accepting the physical sensations associated with anxiety and fear without judgement.
2. Anchoring our reality in the knowledge of our true self instead of the anxious thoughts.
3. Adopting a posture of stillness and knowing.
4. Entering the presence of God.

Do you have a *Memorial*, a *Safe Place*, or a *Spiritual Space* to facilitate entering into the presence of God? If not, I would encourage you to establish one. Where the Father is, there is healing because His presence brings healing. He is Jehovah Rapha. The Lord is my Healer.

13

Transformation of the Mind

To overcome our fear and anxiety disorders and gain lasting freedom, we need to go deep with the Lord in our inner healing. This involves a dive into the recesses of our mind which are a part of our personality. It involves a great degree of honesty, courage, and perseverance. In psychiatry, many of us would only consider treatment to be successful if we can arrive at a point of relapse prevention. To achieve that, we need to consider a patient's risk factors, and their propensity to relapse. In my experience, the greatest risk factor, when it comes to relapse, tends to be a flawed mindset.

For example, people who seek perfection are more likely to develop obsessive compulsive disorder and will remain vulnerable to relapse unless they change their belief that perfection is a necessity. Most will only change once they seek psychotherapy, as they can't easily adjust their thinking without a wider perspective and an understanding of how to change. Similarly, to achieve deep inner healing from anxiety problems and fear, we need a transformation of the mind. We may achieve this when we work with a Christian therapist under the guidance of the Holy Spirit, or when we submit ourselves to God by coming into His presence to seek His help in making a radical change (Philippians 2:13, Romans 12:1-2).

THE MINDSET OF CHRIST

On this side of heaven, sin is not the only thing which hinders our growth and robs us of our ability to live our full potential and achieve our full capacity as God has intended. The author of Hebrews wrote:

> *Therefore, since we are surrounded by such a great cloud of witnesses, let us throw off everything that hinders and the sin that so easily entangles. And let us run with perseverance the race marked out for us.*
>
> — *HEBREWS 12:1*

There are things which hinder us that do not fall into the category of sin. I consider one of these things to be our mindset. The Apostle Paul wrote in Ephesians 4:22-24:

> *You were taught, with regard to your former way of life, to put off your old self, which is being corrupted by its deceitful desires; to be made new in the attitude of your minds; and to put on the new self, created to be like God in true righteousness and holiness.*

Mindset can be defined as a set of beliefs, attitudes, and assumptions that shape how we perceive ourselves, others, and the world around us. Our mindset provides the model or framework through which we interpret our experience with others and the world. Ultimately, it influences the way we relate to other people and the world, and it is a part of our spirituality.

The Apostle Paul encouraged us to have the mindset of Christ by treating one another with humility and love (Philippians 2:5-8). He also said that the spirit of a man illuminates his own mind, while it is the Spirit of God who reveals His thoughts to us:

> *The Spirit searches all things, even the deep things of God. For who knows a person's thoughts except their own spirit within them? In the same way no one knows the thoughts of God except the Spirit of God.*
>
> — *1 CORINTHIANS 2:10-11*

Paul believed we can have the same mindset as Christ. Through the

Holy Spirit revealing the thoughts of God to us, we are enabled to think and perceive in alignment with the values, attitudes, and priorities of Jesus Christ.

What we have received is not the spirit of the world, but the Spirit who is from God, so that we may understand what God has freely given us.
— 1 CORINTHIANS 2:12

The person without the Spirit does not accept the things that come from the Spirit of God but considers them foolishness and cannot understand them because they are discerned only through the Spirit.
— 1 CORINTHIANS 2:14

True Christian spirituality is concerned with matters of the mind because we are encouraged to have the mind of Christ (1 Corinthians 2:16). And having this mind further helps us overcome our anxiety problems and fears.

MINDSETS THAT PROMOTE ANXIETY AND FEAR

I have observed that there are three mindsets which make us vulnerable towards developing anxiety problems and fear. They can also cause us to suffer a relapse after initial healing or even delay our healing. I have also observed this vulnerability is no respecter of religious faith. It operates with a "universal" law, such as gravity which affects Christians and non-Christians alike. Christians don't fly when they tumble off a building. They drop to the ground if there is nothing to break the fall. That is why it is important for all of us, regardless of our faith, to consider and be aware of these dangerous mindsets.

Perfectionism

Perfectionistic people set a very high standard for themselves and others. "But—," you may ask, "—isn't it good to keep improving and seek excellence?" Yes, but there is a difference between seeking improvement and seeking perfectionism. The former has a target and an end goal, but the latter will never be satisfied. Perfectionistic people have no end point, as the goalpost is constantly moving. The standard and yardstick are moved higher and higher as the person drives themselves harder and harder, with such a mindset normally resulting in one of two negative consequences. The first is when, worn out by constant striving and the elusiveness of a good result, the perfectionistic buckles under the constant stress of life. The second consequence is when the person gives up even trying because their standard of perfection is unachievable. Often, a panic attack over these stresses may hit when the person least expects it. Then an anxiety disorder or fear can emerge.

Perfectionism makes it difficult for us to exercise our faith and trust in God. It promotes self-reliance and pushes us to strive for a perfection which does not exist this side of heaven. Perfectionism can rob us from living life in the dimension of grace which knows that it is out of His abundance that we have what we have. Potentially, we become less grateful, which incidentally lowers our mental health. Perfectionists can become quite self-critical for not achieving enough, and eventually their chronic anxiety can lead to severe depression. They are also often critical of others who are "not good enough". At best, their outlook can drive others crazy, and at worst it can lead to severe relationship problems as no one can ever reach the unreasonable standards expected of them.

I have seen many perfectionistic Christians over my lifetime as a psychiatrist, with one young man in particular standing out. He was in Year 11 when he first came under my care as a Mensa kid[15] with an IQ of 140. This young man had been referred to me as, despite his incredible intellect, he was unable to meet deadlines for his schoolwork and projects. He struggled to initiate actual work because he kept thinking about how to present the absolute best answer in his homework or project. He was clearly perfectionistic and very anxious about failing his examinations, and I took the approach of recommending he stretch the last bit of his high school education across three years instead of two. This would help to reduce the stress of his workload and hopefully prevent the inevitable disappointment

---

15 To join Mensa, a social organisation for highly gifted youth and adults, a candidate must score at or above the 98th percentile on a standardised IQ test.

that he had done badly—a disappointment that he would feel regardless of his actual performance, as he would only be happy with utter perfection. With the pressure somewhat mitigated and with free time available, he was able to attend regular psychotherapy sessions with me. I incorporated Christian spirituality in my management of his anxiety, as I challenged him to accept that there is always an element of uncertainty in life—and that this acceptance of uncertainty is what allows us to access God's grace. After two years, he began to show improvement sufficient for him to confidently sit his higher school examination with far less anxiety. He continued to see me for another two years until he had overcome his perfectionism entirely.

'Overstaying' our Time in the Past

Anxiety and fear often stem from uncertainty, perceived threats, or past traumas. Many of us who suffer from anxiety problems overstay our time in the past. There are many reasons for this, but the most common ones are: that the past has paralysed us from moving forward in life; we identify too much with the past; and we hang onto the pain of the past.

Trauma and pain are constant features of this earthly life. Sometimes we perpetrate trauma and pain on ourselves due to our own wrong choices. At other times, others perpetuate trauma and pain onto us, either by design or unintentionally. Repressing or suppressing our response to trauma and pain is detrimental to our mental and spiritual life. The sooner we learn to deal with the trauma and pain, the faster we can move on with our lives. But some of us hang onto the past and won't let go, while others fluctuate between letting go and giving up. Unfortunately, living in the past means that, whenever the person goes back to the past, they are unwittingly re-traumatised. The fight-flight response is once more activated, and over time a chronic anxiety disorder sets in. The fight-flight response remains stubbornly turned on and refuses to be shut down, and the person's life is robbed of joy and freedom. Eventually, they become depressed due to psychological exhaustion.

"Overstaying" in our past can result in us becoming reductionistic in our inner healing journey. Many people get fixated on finding one key event or "root cause" for their fear or anxiety problems. The fact of life is that most issues with anxiety and fear occur due to many different factors converging on us. Not only is this consistent with my knowledge of the spiritual biopsychosocial model of anxiety disorders and fear, but also my personal and professional experiences tell me that our behaviour does not happen in a vacuum. How we respond to problems impacts our environment and even others, who in turn will behave accordingly. Our study of Jacob's fear testifies to that.

Hanging onto the past not only results in more pain, it also changes our positive self-identity. Soon, we define ourselves by our anxiety problems and fear, as I see in patients who introduce themselves with "I am a schizophrenic" or "I am bipolar". Christians can also reflect this poor self-identity when we constantly say, "I am a sinner saved by grace" rather than "I am a beloved child of God ". Preoccupation with our pain not only increases it but also robs us of realising our true potential. Above all, it nullifies the sovereignty of God. We need to learn to "forget the former things and not dwell on the past" (Isaiah 43:18) so that we can move on to the more excellent future God has designed for us:

> *I do not consider myself yet to have taken hold of it. But one thing I do: Forgetting what is behind and straining toward what is ahead, I press on toward the goal to win the prize for which God has called me heavenward in Christ Jesus.*
>
> — *Philippians 3:13-14*

Freedom from anxiety problems and fear is about stepping out of the prison cell of the past and purposely moving towards our true potential. This is the transformed mindset.

Hyper-focussing on the Future

Remember the movie "Back to the Future" starring Michael J Fox, which was released in 1985? Despite its age, it remains a well-known cult classic, and some of us who are of a younger generation may have watched it on Netflix.

While the movie is highly entertaining, it is also deeply philosophical. It explores the idea of time travel and ties that in with the tension of fate versus free will. The main character, Marty McFly, journeys back in time to the 1950s and then forward to the 1980s, hoping to change certain events in the past in order to improve his future. Ultimately, he discovers that some aspects of destiny are unchangeable. The movie suggests that we have the power to make choices for our future, but we have limited ability to alter the course of history.

Most of us have entertained the fantasy idea of time travel. It seems to be a universal phenomenon and is a common theme in many science-fiction movies. On a spiritual level, I believe it is also a misplaced desire to be God-like. Like Marty, we want to know the future in order to control it. Our fantasy to be all-knowing is a replay of the scene in the Garden of Eden where the serpent tells Eve that humans can be "like God" (Genesis 3:5). When we are too preoccupied with the future, we miss out on the present. We eliminate our need for connection with God and others, and we become more anxious. Constantly living in the future means we no longer do life with God in the present. But Jesus commands us: "Do not worry about tomorrow, for tomorrow will worry about itself. Each day has enough trouble of its own" (Matthew 6:34).

Feeling uncertain about the future breeds worry, and worries breed anxiety and fear. Studies show that about 85% of our worries do not become reality. They only exist in our mind, but even there they are detrimental to our mental well-being. The Lord's Prayer (Matthew 6:9-13) provides a remedy for our worries:

1. Begin the day with a connection to God our Father through an attitude of worship: "Our Father in heaven, hallowed be your name." (verse 9)

2. Orientate your life towards the Kingdom of our Father: "Your kingdom come, your will be done, on earth as it is in heaven." (verse 10)

3. Be assured that our Father looks after our daily physical needs: "Give us today our daily bread." (verse 11)

4. Be assured of His grace towards us: "And forgive us our debts, as we also have forgiven our debtors." (verse 12)

5. Be assured that He looks after our spiritual needs: "And lead us not into temptation but deliver us from the evil one." (verse 13)

In your quest for freedom from anxiety problems and fear, use the Lord's Prayer to transform your mind. When you step into your *Safe Place* (see Chapter 12), meditate on this prayer, recite it, and see clearly in your mind the reality of the points in the prayer until your spirit is encouraged. Use the assurances in the Lord's Prayer when you are in your *Spiritual Space* (see Chapter 12) as you go about your day. Keep referencing back to key points in between the busy schedules of your life.

A SPIRITUAL PROGRAM TOWARDS A TRANSFORMED MIND

Research in psychology suggests that forming new habits, or altering ingrained patterns of behaviour, typically takes several weeks to several months of consistent practice and reinforcement. However, changing an underlying mindset may require ongoing reflection, self-awareness, and therapeutic interventions over a longer period.

It's important to approach the process of change with patience, self-compassion, and a willingness to seek support from trusted individuals or professionals when needed. While change may not happen overnight, it is possible with dedication, persistence, and a commitment to personal growth and development. We need a plan which incorporates Christian spirituality to reach a true transformation of our mindset. I offer one program below which I have used with good success:

I use Philippians 4:4-9 as the basic blueprint for a transformed mind to gain freedom from anxiety and fear:

Rejoice in the Lord always. I will say it again: Rejoice! Let your gentleness be evident to all. The Lord is near. Do not be anxious about anything, but in every situation, by prayer and petition, with thanksgiving, present your requests to God. And the peace of God, which transcends all understanding, will guard your hearts and your minds in Christ Jesus. Finally, brothers and sisters, whatever is true, whatever is noble, whatever is right, whatever is pure, whatever is lovely, whatever is admirable—if anything is excellent or praiseworthy—think about such things. Whatever you have learned or received or heard from me or seen in me—put it into practice. And the God of peace will be with you.

Making A Radical Decision to Rejoice

Transformation of the mind begins with a decision to rejoice. I define rejoicing as an outward manifestation of inner contentment, reflecting a sense of gratitude and appreciation for life's blessings. It is a state of choosing to be satisfied with our current circumstances or situation and surrendering our difficult situations to God, knowing that ultimately we are held in His loving care, and trusting that no matter what happens, His higher purpose for us will be fulfilled.

Contentment allows us to cease striving. It is different from happiness which is an emotional response to a real or perceived positive experience in our life. In our struggles with fear and anxiety, we have to make a radical decision to access a feeling of contentment. Contentment ties us closely with *shalom*—the deep, internal peace that comes from knowing that we are held in God's embrace.

Reminding Ourselves Not to be Anxious

In all of life, practice makes perfect. Choosing to stick to any program is a difficult decision to make. It is an act of our will. By the time our anxiety and fear are chronic, it is difficult to persevere. It is much easier to just give in to your anxiety and fear and let them roll. Indeed, many of my patients—Christians and non-Christians alike—tell me, "Kam, it is difficult to fight. It is so exhausting! I usually just give up."

However, if we choose to be tenacious about sticking to a program, we can slowly overcome our anxiety. Hopefully, by the time you arrive at this chapter, you have practised the skills of being aware of your anxious feelings without reacting to them, anchoring your mind on a positive statement or personal experience (or a Bible verse which promotes calm and peace), adopting a spiritual posture of stillness and knowing God, and actively entering into the presence of God. Any of these skills by themselves or in combination—with practice—will help you to be less anxious.

Taking Our Fear and Anxiety Back to God

We can take our fear and anxiety back to God with "prayer and petition, with thanksgiving" (Philippians 4:6). To me, prayer is a personal way of communicating with God and can include expressions of gratitude, praise, worship, confession, and requests. A petition is a more specific type of communication, focusing on intervention, assistance, guidance, or blessing.

In the journey to the transformation of our minds, we need to engage with God constantly. Prayer is not a one-sided request to God of our wants or needs, but a bidirectional, two-way communication. If we read the account of Jacob wrestling with God (Genesis 32:22-32) as symbolic of prayer, then we will get a good picture of prayer. It is a personal, life-changing encounter with God, through which we "hear" the voice of God, and it happens in our *Safe Place* or *Spiritual Space* (see Chapter 12).

Our prayer needs to end with thanksgiving because a true encounter with God changes our life for the better. In the case of healing from our fear and anxiety, we need to have faith that it is a done deal. Like Jacob, we need to recognise our encounters with God and, after each episode, recognise how our mind has further been transformed. We also need to record it so that we can remember it in the future. We may not set up a stone pillar *Memorial*, but we can journal our experience with God. I always encourage my patients to keep a "healing journal" so that they are aware of how much improvement they have made.

CULTIVATE A HEALTHY MINDSET

If we want our mind transformed, not only do we need to remove an unhelpful diet of anxious and fearful thoughts and beliefs, but we also need to add life-giving and positive "foods" such as anything that is true, honourable, right, pure, lovely, admirable, excellent, or worthy of praise (Philippians 4:8). I call this the healthy mind diet. A healthy mind is a transformed mind, and a transformed mind is no longer a breeding place for anxiety and fear.

If we want to have a transformed mind, we need to identify Bible verses which encourage us not to fear or be anxious and meditate on these daily. Some of these verses could be Isaiah 43:1, 41:10, 41:13-14; 1 John 4:18; Matthew 6:28, 6:31; and Luke 12:22. These are just some of my favourite verses, but you may have your own personal repertoire.

You can incorporate meditation of these verses in the exercises *Be Still and Know* and *The Presence*.

PRACTICE AND PRACTICE

The Apostle Paul admonished his readers to put into action what he taught them (Philippians 4:9), and I would do likewise. A truth is not alive until you walk it out. At the beginning of this chapter, I noted that changing our mindset—which is our internal working model—takes time. Whatever age we are, that is the duration of time that we have had an internal working model guiding us to feel and behave fearfully and anxiously. It took Jacob a good twenty years to overcome his fear (Genesis 27-33), and while I am not saying we should all take this long, I want to encourage you that healing can take longer than expected. We simply need to persevere.

Victory is a cumulation of many little successes, until we can reach a certain threshold and find ourselves on a new trajectory. This is when we truly have the peace of God (Philippians 4:9). When we reach that moment in time, we reach our sabbath. We are no longer motivated by strife but by rest, and we welcome a deep sense of *shalom*. We experience true contentment, and we are rich in our spirit and prosperous in our soul. That is when we realise that our Father is a redemptive God and that nothing is wasted in the economy of His Kingdom. Whatever the locusts have eaten, He will return manyfold to us (Joel 2:25).

14

Looking Into the Father's Face

Scrape below the surface of the fear and anxiety problems we are battling, and soon we will be confronted with our core issues relating to our inner needs. These inner needs help to express our humanity, and chief amongst these are the needs for security and significance. Parents who have the well-being of their offspring in mind, normally parent their children in such a way as to meet those needs by protecting, providing, and maintaining the physical, emotional, psychological, and social needs of their children. Disruption of parenting due to circumstances such as neglect and abuse, or circumstances external to the parents' control such as illness, tragedy, separation and wars, result in an inability to meet the needs of the child.

The unmet need for security and significance often results in various types of anxiety disorders and fear. When we consult a psychiatrist, our problems may not be entirely remitted by a prescription for medication or various psychological therapies to help repair our broken emotions and maladaptive behaviours. We will not achieve full recovery until we confront our unmet inner needs.

SEEING OUR MOTHER'S FACE

As a trainee psychiatrist, I was taught about the many different schools of psychotherapy. One school was Self Psychology which resonated well with me. Self Psychology is a psychoanalytic approach developed by Heinz Kohut in the mid-20th century.[16] Self Psychology posits that, as infants, we lack a cohesive sense of self.

It is through interactions with our mother, who expresses her emotions through her face, that we begin to develop a more integrated and coherent sense of self. If our mother's face mirrors our emotions accurately, it affirms and validates us, fostering a feeling of security and stability. For example, when still at that preverbal stage of development, as babies we express our needs through crying or other distressed behaviour. Our mother uses her emotions to empathically "tune in" to our emotions, and then responds accordingly with facial expressions and words of assurance, actively bringing comfort and nurturing to us. When we "read" the caring emotions on our mother's face and receive her comfort, we experience a sense of relief from our distress. Our needs are met, and we feel understood. The positive outcome from this interaction between infant and mother reinforces to us that our emotions are valid, we are valued, and we are positively and unconditionally loved. This helps to build a sense of self-worth. But when our mother ignores us or responds in a negative or inappropriate fashion, we feel invalidated and unaffirmed, and eventually we grow up with little or poor self-worth.

Through the mirroring and unconditional love of a mother, an infant grows a deep attachment to her. They feel a sense of "like" towards their mother and they want to be like her. Indeed, for those of us who received positive and unconditional love from our mother, she is often our first love "object". Our mother offers inspiration and guidance in our identity formation with a sense of significance, and it is not unusual that many of us, once we are adults, still turn to our mother for help and comfort when we are in difficulty. Mothers hold such a special place in our hearts.

In secular analytic psychotherapy, our patients share with us their difficulties, problems, and concerns. We then use our empathy to accurately attune to the patient's emotional state and distress. We are non-judgemental,

---

16 Kohut, H. (1971). *The Analysis of the Self: A Systematic Approach to the Psychoanalytic Treatment of Narcissistic Personality Disorders.* International Universities Press.

non-critical, and hold a positive regard for the patient. In this sense, we step into the place of a mother, reflecting back to the patient what is in their unconscious mind. In this way, we help the patient to "repair" the sense of self which has been damaged. However, my experience is that many patients are still left with a hollow place in their hearts. The intellectual understanding that our anxiety problems and fear are a result of non-optimal parenting, and the warmth, empathy, and acceptance of our therapist, somehow still prove insufficient to fill the vacuum in our hearts. I think the real problem is that therapists can have unconditional acceptance for our patients, but we cannot love them unconditionally the way a parent would.

SEEING OUR FATHER'S FACE

Since the day of Sigmund Freud—who is regarded as the father of psychoanalysis—psychiatrists and analysts have keenly studied the relationship between mother and baby. In most, if not all, cultures, and since time immemorial, the mother has been the primary caregiver. However, this is not to say the father does not play a role in the baby's life. All of us have a hierarchy of intimate relationships, and in a modern industrialised society with the preponderance of a nuclear family, the father is equally important as the mother. Since the father also plays a very significant role in the normal and healthy development of a baby, the father-infant relationship also contributes to the child's validation, affirmation, and establishment of a healthy sense of self-worth, as well as the development of an integrated and coherent sense of self.

Sad to say, many of us live a life in which our father is absent. This is especially true considering we have had two world wars within the last century. The Second World War alone—which lasted from 1939 to 1945—was one of the deadliest conflicts in human history, resulting in immense human suffering on a global scale and the loss of life of seventy to eighty-five million, many of them men. Of the men who survived, both military and civilians suffered from post-traumatic stress disorder which affected their parenting. Poorly parented children internalise poor parenting skills, and this results in a cycle of disadvantage where psychologically impaired fathers parent children who then parent the next generation. The generation of inadequately parented "children" is large indeed if we consider that many nations have also gone through civil wars in the last century. Globalisation further results in the phenomenon of "the absent father", as many fathers have to spend a great deal of time overseas to make a living. The result of these experiences is that many of us do not get sufficient validation and affirmation when we look into our father's face. This leaves us with a sense of inner emptiness. We may try to replace and fill our inner void with the pursuit of power, prestige, and wealth, but none of these ever speak to us with words like "You are worthwhile," "I am so proud of you," and "I love you."

BEHOLDING JESUS' FACE

During my years as a psychotherapist, I have discovered a truth: Our sense of significance, self-worth and legitimacy is given and nurtured by our parents during our developmental years. When we don't have it, or we have it in a distorted form, it is hard to replace. It cannot be filled by our achievements, but some of us may find some healing in significant others such as a benevolent and kind parental figure or a life partner. Our humanity is best expressed when we are loved and valued by looking into a person who truly loves us for who we are and not for what we do.

No wonder the Bible encourages us to look into the face of God. In the book of Psalms, David the king wrote, "My heart says of you, 'Seek his face!' Your face, Lord, I will seek" (Psalm 27:8) and "Let your face shine on your servant; save me in your unfailing love" (Psalm 31:16).

Our best example, however, is Jesus, who came primarily to show us the face of God, and what it means to look into His face as our "Abba" (or, personally intimate) Father.

The Parable of the Rich Young Ruler
Let's consider a Bible story found in the Gospel of Mark[17]:

17 This story is also recorded in Matthew 19:16-26 and in Luke 18:18-27.

As Jesus started on his way, a man ran up to him and fell on his knees before him. "Good teacher," he asked, "what must I do to inherit eternal life?"

"Why do you call me good?" Jesus answered. "No one is good—except God alone. You know the commandments: "You shall not murder, you shall not commit adultery, you shall not steal, you shall not give false testimony, you shall not defraud, honour your father and mother."

"Teacher," he declared, "all these I have kept since I was a boy."

Jesus looked at him and loved him. "One thing you lack," he said. "Go, sell everything you have and give to the poor, and you will have treasure in heaven. Then come, follow me."

At this the man's face fell. He went away sad because he had great wealth.

— MARK 10:17-22

This "Story of the Rich Young Ruler" introduces us to a man of power and great wealth. In today's society, he would probably be considered a global elite—the top 0.1% of the population. This incredibly wealthy man was a law-abiding citizen who had kept the commandments of God since he was a young boy. But there was something missing in his life. Unlike the Pharisees and the lawyers during his time, he was deeply aware that something was missing, and he came to Jesus with a deep sense of reverence to enquire as to how he could inherit eternal life. He knew that eternal life cannot be bought. It is a gift.

Let us imagine for a moment that we were there, two thousand years ago. Better still, let us imagine ourselves to be the rich, young ruler as we immerse ourselves in the exchange between Jesus and this man:

We read that "Jesus looked at the young man and loved him" (verse 21). There was a connectedness between the two, and when he looked into Jesus' face, he felt that love—an emotion which involves but also surpasses compassion. Jesus looked at the young man and connected with his heart, his inner void, and his sincere desire to have that void filled. And He responded by asking the man to sell what he had, give to the poor, and follow Him.

Contrary to some interpretations, I don't believe for a moment that

Jesus wanted to stump this man or call him out. No, Jesus loved him indeed, so He suggested a more excellent way for the man to invest his wealth. An investment into the heavenly treasure chest where no "moths and vermin destroy, and thieves break in and steal" (Matthew 6:19). Jesus also extended an invitation to the young man to follow Him. He wanted the young man to do life with Him, just like the disciples. Jesus saw the potential in this young man, just as He sees great potential in each of us. He loved this man so much that He wanted him to inherit eternal life, which is a deep and intimate relationship with Father God and with Jesus Himself.

> *And this is eternal life: that they may know you, the only true God, and Jesus Christ, whom you have sent.*
>
> *— JOHN 17:3*

This rich young ruler would have inherited it all had he chosen life with Jesus. He would have also fulfilled the potential he was created for, but I surmise that—like a lot of wealthy people—the rich young ruler had anxiety and fear over losing his wealth. Such is the irony of life! We fret when we are poor. We fret when we are rich.

Yet love is so powerful that when it is given to us, and when we choose to receive it, it brings out the best and most excellent in us.

When we look into Jesus' face, we cannot help but see His love for us. It is as though we are looking into Abba Father's face. Jesus was, in essence, sent to us to bring us to the Father.

> *Jesus answered, "I am the way and the truth and the life. No one comes to the Father except through me. If you really know me, you will know my Father as well. From now on, you do know him and have seen him."*
>
> *— JOHN 14:6-7*

At the end of the day, we must deal with our unmet or distorted inner needs for security and significance, self-worth and a sense of legitimacy, by coming to our Abba Father and looking into His face. As a therapist, when my Christian patients reach the stage of addressing their inner needs, I introduce Abba Father into the therapeutic space we share. I seek to mirror Abba Father's love, validation, and affirmation to my patient. I become the milepost between my patient and Abba Father, the objective being for them to find their own integrated and coherent sense of self in Abba Father. After all, Abba Father invented the parent-child relationship because He is the first prototypical parent (Malachi 2:10, Ephesians 4:6 and Acts 17:28-29).

BEHOLDING THE FACE OF GOD

In the Hebraic tradition, beholding God's face is a moment of great spiritual significance and encompasses experiencing His presence, favour, intimacy, and revelation. It indicates a profound encounter with the divine that cannot help but shape one's spiritual journey and understanding of God's nature and purposes. God spoke to Moses face to face (Exodus 33:11), and Moses asked to see the face of God (Exodus 33:20-23). The Lord also instructed Aaron and his sons to bless the children of Israel with the Aaronic blessing:

> *The Lord bless you and keep you; the Lord make his face shine upon you, and be gracious to you; the Lord lift up his countenance upon you, and give you peace.*
>
> — *Numbers 6:24-26*

I believe that we have not emphasised enough this aspect of our Christian spirituality, and it is seldom explored in Christian teaching. If looking into our parents' faces is so vital for human development and our sense of self, how much more valuable, in our development as children of God, that we can look into Abba Father's face?

Some years ago, my wife and I had the privilege of visiting St Petersburg in Russia. During our trip, we visited the famous Hermitage Museum. I was looking forward to seeing the painting by the Dutch artist Rembrandt van Rijn called "Return of the Prodigal Son". The painting depicts the biblical parable of the prodigal son's return to his father after squandering his inheritance and living a life of excess. In the painting, the father embraces his son tenderly while the son kneels before his father in repentance and humility. The composition captures the moment of forgiveness, reconciliation, and unconditional love, conveying themes of redemption, mercy, and the transformative power of grace. I spent a great deal of time gazing at this painting, trying to immerse myself in the scene. I was struck with how magnanimous the father appeared. Indeed, that is how Father God seemed to me when I first returned to Him, many years earlier. I saw the painting from the son's perspective. Reflecting on it now, I wonder if someone might one day paint a matching piece, this time from the father's perspective as he looks into his son's face with unconditional love, affirmation and validation that "You are indeed my son!"

The Parable of the Prodigal Son

The story of the prodigal son is a very well-known parable of Jesus. It is the story of a generous father and his two sons. This parable holds a wonderful message of salvation, but I believe it also holds great truth in regard to our inner need for security and significance. The parable of the prodigal son teaches us a lot about our own mental health.

The story is told in Luke 15:11-32. It begins with the younger son of a rich man asking for his share of his father's estate. We are not told the reasons for his request, but perhaps, being the second-born, he felt insignificant. His older brother had the birthright and would inherit a double portion of their father's estate, assuming the position of leadership and authority in the family. So he made his request, and his father duly gave him his portion of inheritance.

The younger son travelled incognito to a country far away, with the intention of making it by himself. He wanted to establish his own identity outside of simply being the younger son. With the wealth he was given, he might have gained some sense of significance—indeed, wealth and positions of power often make us noteworthy in the eyes of the world. But the young man used his wealth foolishly and soon found himself dead broke and working a job that was the lowest of the low—feeding pigs. His significance was at an all-time low. Nobody wanted to know him. His mood was as low as his social status. He had hit rock bottom. At this point, the young man realised that even being a servant to his wealthy but kind and just father would mean he was better off. Full of shame, he decided he had no other choice but to return home. His heart was heavy, burdened by a sense of illegitimacy. He wondered if his father would let him become one of his servants, or if he would turn his son away in disgust. Nevertheless, the man began the long journey home in his pitiful state, filthy and destitute.

Unbeknown to the son, his father had been waiting daily for his return. When the young man was still some way from the house, the father spotted him in the distance. Before he could even reach his family home, his father had rushed out to embrace him and kiss him passionately. The young man desperately wanted to recount to his father the full measure of his unworthiness and his sins, but his father wanted only to delight in the safe return of his son. Servants were commanded to clothe the son with the best robe, putting a ring on his finger and sandals on his bare and broken feet. Then his father hosted a huge banquet—the best that had been seen—to welcome his son home. It was a celebration like no other.

Meanwhile, the eldest son soon came home from a hard day's work in the fields. He heard the joyful sound of music, songs, and dances, and when he queried the servants, they told him that his father had thrown a big party to celebrate the safe homecoming of his younger brother. The eldest son was so furious he refused to join in, and his father pleaded with him to no avail. He complained bitterly: "I have worked for you so hard for so long. I feel like a slave. I dare not disobey you. Yet I don't feel secure that you will give me a little something to celebrate with my mates. Now, this horrible son of yours has squandered away your wealth in sins, and yet you throw such as big party!"

His father replied, "Son, you and I are always together. Everything I have is yours. All my wealth is at your disposal. But we need to celebrate your brother. He did not understand what it meant to be a son. But now he does!"

Notice that *both sons* expressed unmet needs for security and significance, which resulted in low self-worth. Like many of us, the eldest son used hard work and legalism to achieve his self-worth. But the more he tried this route, the more insecure he felt. He was blind to the reality that, as the firstborn son, he held all the blessings of the birthright. He suffered from a sense of illegitimacy because he behaved and acted like a slave, even though this was not asked of him. His emphasis on hard work and legalism resulted in a lack of joy and much fear. He dared not use even a teensy-weensy bit of his father's resources, and he channelled his fear into deeply repressed anger towards his father. He felt that his father did not celebrate him as he deserved.

Meanwhile the younger son, like many of us, decided he could do better without the father. He wanted to make it on his own, but the irony is that he needed his father's wealth in order to take that road. The younger son had nothing, and he used his father's wealth to meet his inner need for significance. But when that wealth was lost, he also lost the fake sense of significance he had cultivated. The younger son also suffered from a sense of illegitimacy, but his came from losing connection with his father. This resulted in a loss of self-worth and profound feelings of shame. His shame made him blind to the reality that, despite his poor decisions and disastrous circumstances, his father could and would still meet his needs for security and significance, reestablishing his self-worth.

Looking Into Our Father's Face for Healing of Our Unmet Inner Needs

I have noticed that many societies in the Far East are characterised by "father absenteeism". As I teach about mental health in these countries, I am always amazed at the response people show when they are introduced to the love of God, their Father. The joy of seeing elderly men and women weep and dance as they learn to gaze into their heavenly father's face and respond to the touch of the Holy Spirit is indescribable. The same is true for many of my Christian patients when they begin to realise that God is not far from them, He is not displeased or angry or aloof—quite the contrary. His heart yearns for His children, and He is patiently longing for us to share His embrace. I have seen countless people set free from longstanding mental health problems and deep sadness as they find their true worth and identity in the face of their heavenly father.

SPIRITUAL EXERCISES FOR LOOKING INTO OUR FATHER'S FACE

Exercise One: Getting to Know Our Abba Father

1. Adopt a spiritual posture of "Be Still and Know", then read the *Parable of the Prodigal Son* in Luke 15:11-32 as though this is the first time you have come across it.
2. Ask Abba Father to show His face to you. List the characteristics of Abba Father in your own words.
3. Compare with the list below to see if there is any concurrence:

   - He is rich in mercy, kindness, and love (v. 12)
   - He is ready, willing, and able to heal (v. 20)
   - He can do exceedingly, abundantly, above and beyond what we expect from our restoration (v. 22-23)
   - There is always a restart with Abba Father (v. 24)
   - He is with us at all times (v. 31)
   - Everything He has is mine (v. 31)

4. In your *Safe Place* or *Spiritual Space* (see Chapter 12), invite Abba Father to show you a deeper knowledge of His loving kindness and goodness.
5. Journal your spiritual experience.
6. Maintain a sense of your *Spiritual Space* in your daily routine, being receptive to Abba Father as He reveals His goodness in your daily activities. You may like to declare the truths you discovered from the *Parable of the Prodigal Son* over yourself, e.g.:

   "I declare that my Abba Father is rich in mercy, kindness, and love. He is ready, willing, and able to heal. He can do exceedingly abundantly above and beyond what I expect for my restoration. There is always a restart with Abba Father. He is always with me, and everything He has is mine."

You can also declare the Aaronic blessing from Numbers 6:24-26 over yourself, e.g.:

"The Lord blesses me and keeps me. The Lord makes His face shine upon me and is gracious to me. The Lord lifts His countenance upon me and gives me peace."

Exercise Two: Looking to Our Abba Father to Meet Our Inner Needs

1. Prayerfully read the *Parable of the Prodigal Son* as though you are reading it for the first time.
2. Consider the truth that our needs can be met in Abba Father:

   - The best robe: A symbol of righteousness which meets our need for *security* (verse 22).
   - The ring: A symbol of Abba Father's delegated authority and power which meets our need for *significance.*
   - The sandals: A luxury only reserved for Abba Father's children, which meets our need for *self-worth.*

3. In your *Safe Place*, ask Abba Father to reveal to you how He meets your need for security, significance, and self-worth. You might like to immerse yourself in the following Psalms:

   - Psalm 23 (for security)
   - Psalm 8 (for significance)
   - Psalm 139:13-18 (for self-worth)

Keep in your spirit's consciousness the following "anchoring" verses:

   - For security: The Lord is my Shepherd, I lack nothing (Psalm 23:1).

- For significance: You have crowned me with glory and honour (Psalm 8:5).
- For self-worth: I am fearfully and wonderfully made and your thoughts of me are vast (Psalm 139:14, 17).

4. Ask Abba Father to show you His goodness in your daily routine and in the tasks that you perform. Then, at the end of each day, with a heart of gratitude, thank Abba Father that He has met your needs in the daily activities you have undertaken.

Exercise Three: Looking Into Our Father's Face to Behold Our Legitimacy

Like the two brothers, our unmet inner needs can give rise to a sense of illegitimacy. We may strive to obtain wealth and positions of power to cover our need to feel secure and significant. But often there is still an inner void which results in shame and anger, and we walk around with a low sense of self-worth. People around us are puzzled, thinking that if only they had what we have, they would be so happy. Indeed, in my practice, I come across many wealthy and highly accomplished patients who walk tall but feel so small inside. Unable to overcome a sense of inner shame, they feel like a fake. For my Christian patients, I journey with them in their therapy, specifically looking into the Father's face for healing. You can also do this spiritual exercise in your own *Safe Place*:

1. Maintain a spiritual posture of stillness with an anticipation to look into the Father's face.
2. Prayerfully read the *Parable of the Prodigal Son* as though it is the first time. See if you can identify with the two brothers and their sense of illegitimacy.
3. Invite the Holy Spirit to reveal to you how you feel in your spirit; whether there is any shame, anger, or rage.
4. Invite the Holy Spirit to minister the words of the Father to you: "You are always with me, and everything I have is yours." (verse 31)

5. Immerse your spirit in the truth of Father's statement.
6. Ask Abba Father to show you His goodness in your daily life. Then, in your daily routine, be consciously aware whenever you are shown evidence of the Father's goodness. You might like to journal your experience.
7. Finally, acknowledge the Father's goodness with gratitude before you go to bed at night.

~

One patient of mine, when he asked Abba Father to show His goodness, felt he was being led to a big barn house and Jesus was there. He understood this to mean he is an heir of the Father, like Jesus. Another patient saw herself in a garden with Abba Father when she looked into the Father's face.

As for me, when I looked into Abba Father's face, I saw Him singing over me. This happened some years ago when I attended a retreat for inner healing in a well-known healing centre in Sydney. It was a full weekend affair from Friday evening to late Sunday afternoon, and I shared a motel-type room with three other attendees. When I first checked into the room, no one was there, but on my bed was a Bible verse:

> *The Lord your God is with you, the Mighty Warrior who saves. He will take great delight in you; in his love he will no longer rebuke you, but will rejoice over you with singing.*
>
> — *ZEPHANIAH 3:17*

Almost immediately, my spirit caught a vision of Abba Father dancing and singing over me in the most celebratory and exuberant mood. I rejected it at the time as irreverent, if not blasphemous. But the moving image has stayed in the mind of my spirit ever since. As though Abba Father has etched it into my spirit. This incident predated my realisation that, much like the older brother in the parable, I was obtaining my sense of legitimacy through hard work and legalism. Abba Father anticipated my later spiritual experience and was preparing my spirit for it. Such is Abba's compassion.

These days, whenever I enter into my *Spiritual Space* and look into His face, I see Abba Father's celebration of me. Now, I try to live life out of the abundance of His grace and peace as "He makes His face shine upon me and lifts His countenance upon me" (Numbers 6:24-26).

So, what do you see when you look into Abba Father's face? He has a huge heart and His thoughts of us are more numerous than the grains of sand on the seashore (Psalm 139:17-18). What do you know about His heart for you, when you peel away the anxiety problems, fear, and unmet inner needs?

I believe that, deep in our being, all of us have a need to see the face of Abba Father; to experience His affirmation, validation, and pleasure in us, and to know that we are worthwhile. Paradoxically, our anxiety problems and fear, painful as they may be, lead us through a journey of healing towards the final destination of seeing the face of Abba Father—of knowing He is eternally good (Exodus 33:18-19), and He has called us to be His children. This is when our theology becomes personal revelation—when we understand in a very deep way that we are intimately connected with Christ, Christ is intimately in union with the Father and us, and we are intimately in union with our Abba Father (John 14:20). This is our ultimate freedom from anxiety problems and fear.

About the Author

Kam's first love was obstetrics but, due to the arduous lifestyle of an obstetrician and upon the encouragement of his professor, Kam decided to specialise in psychiatry instead. His love for working with children and young people led him to the subspecialty of child and adolescent psychiatry, and he has never looked back since. Kam enjoys his work and feels privileged to be a voice of positive influence in his patients' lives.

Kam is married to his wife, Gracia, who is a retired medical practitioner. They have two married adult children and three beautiful granddaughters. Outside his work, Kam enjoys reading, learning new languages, cooking, growing vegetables, travelling and exploring nature with Gracia, and spending time with his family. He conducts prayer ministry with Gracia both in Sydney and overseas. He is a great believer in mission and is involved in teaching psychiatry and prayer ministry in Sydney and in areas overseas such as South East Asia and the Far East.

Kam believes in the empowerment of the individual and in self-help. He shares his mental health knowledge and ongoing learnings with the general public at **www.healthymindconcepts.com.** He also has a dedicated website to explore the subject of mental health and spirituality: **www.drkamwong.com.**

Kam hopes to spend more time writing books to further share his knowledge and experience outside of his clinical practice. He can be contacted at: **drwong@drkamwong.com.**

Healthy Mind Concepts

Dr. Kam Wong has an online presence through his website—**healthymindconcepts.com**—offering free educational articles pertaining to mental health matters, along with a range of Apps such as the Anxiety Toolkit, Distressing Emotions Toolkit, Stress Toolkit, Calm Optimizer, and others, for a range of mental health problems. These are not a substitute for clinical treatment of mental health problems by mental health professionals, but they are useful self-help tools to complement treatment. They are designed for those who are interested in taking a more proactive role in the management of their mental health.

Acknowledgements

I wish to acknowledge the invaluable support I have received from my dear wife, Gracia, in writing this book. Gracia is a pillar of strength for me. She has encouraged me constantly in my Christian ministries, and she is my best intercessor in my endeavours and my life. Thank you, Gracia, for introducing me to prayer ministry, both on the receiving end and the giving end. It is a joy to share our calling in mission and prayer ministry here in Sydney and overseas. Thank you for your steadfastness.